I SING THE SONG OF MYSELF

An Anthology of
Autobiographical Poems

Edited by
DAVID KHERDIAN

I SING THE SONG OF MYSELF

GREENWILLOW BOOKS
A Division of
William Morrow & Company, Inc.
New York

First Edition   10 9 8 7 6 5 4 3 2 1

Library of Congress Cataloging in Publication Data
Main entry under title: I sing the song of myself.
Includes indexes. Summary: A collection of autobiograph-
ical poems by modern American poets.   1. Children's
poetry, American.   2. American poetry—20th century.
[1. American poetry—Collections]   I. Kherdian, David.
PN6110.C4I24   811′.5′408   78-5807
ISBN 0-688-80172-2   ISBN 0-688-84172-4 lib. bdg.

To the memory of Walt Whitman

The poetry of the self; the poetry of the spirit; the poetry of
man in his time and in his skin has been with us from
the beginning of this particular form. Poetry, more than
any other art, has as its domain the person of the writer.
It is for this reason that the reading of poetry can become
a special experience and adventure, because when the
poet's own true story is actually/artfully told, it becomes
everyman's story. And it is this special quality of
familiarity and warmth that can make a participant of
the reader. The poet may be a specialist in language, but
nothing could be more common—more universal and
important—than the theme of his work: Man.

Whether as he is or as he wants to be, the poet is,
in this very moment—as he comes to us writing/speaking
these poems—just himself, just you, just me.

DAVID KHERDIAN

Canby, Oregon
August 26, 1977

Autobiographia Literaria

FRANK O'HARA

When I was a child
I played by myself in a
corner of the schoolyard
all alone.

I hated dolls and I
hated games, animals were
not friendly and birds
flew away.

If anyone was looking
for me I hid behind a
tree and cried out "I am
an orphan."

And here I am, the
center of all beauty!
writing these poems!
Imagine!

Contents

The First Poem I Ever Wrote

NAOMI SHIHAB

I was not divinely inspired,
I was excited,
at six many things were new, fresh,
they still are,
then they were even newer,
to me.
I'm speaking for myself.

At six
speaking for myself
was new.

I lived in St. Louis,
banks of the Mississippi,
Gateway to the West,
it was my place,
the only place,
even though my father was an Arab
I thought the whole world lived in Missouri,
I thought everybody knew everybody,
I was absolutely positive
everybody knew me.

We took a trip to Chicago, on a train,
my father had business in Chicago,
I had business in Chicago,
I had a poem waiting for me,
it would be there when I got off the train,
watching for me, shyly,
behind the tracks of the Elevated Railway,
inside the starred dome of the planetarium,
at the corner where the streets went up
to make channels for the boats.
It would disguise itself as the faces passing,
the odd faces, the twisted faces,
the sad hopeful faces I had never seen before
though they were part of me, all of them,
I was more than a neighborhood,
I was a city, a big city,
a city I would explore forever,
and that was the poem.

Genus Hylobates

JIM GIBBONS

since grammar school i remember kids laughing
especially joyce and donald because my name
is gibbons yes gibbons not gibbon there is a
difference gibbon is a small slender long-armed
arboreal anthropoid ape of the genus hylobates
found in the east indies and southern asia
and gibbons or me is just a normal child like
anyone who has flipped baseball cards during
recess or stolen balloons from winkies to make
their bike sound like a real motorcycle or
maybe just fill with water and whip at cars
after school and though i have hung from trees
which may have stretched my arms a little
they do not drag between my legs when i walk
nor can i scratch my back with my left arm
by way of my crotch while hanging from my right
or even feel comfortable thinking about it and
i did not attend the annual monkey convention
in salem massachushetts or even receive any kind
of notice or brochure pertaining to it or would
have even considered it if i had as i am taller
than twenty-four inches although i know how it
feels to be small and getting my ass kicked from
all the big apes in the neighborhood but i did
not attack janet cox of glendale california or
even hear about it via the grapevine or any other
kind of vine but read about it in the paper and
besides violence and bananas do not appeal to me
as a steady diet except maybe if they are used
in the appropriate capacity to possibly raise an
individual to a higher or better state of being.

Turning 30 Poem

JOHN BRANDI

I am turning thirty
today half cloudy wheels spinning home alone splitting wood
plucking nopales wife out shopping for crunchy granola
kids down the creek splashing dough rising in the porcelain sink
I am turning thirty

Suddenly sunday by myself standing in front of the mirror
trying to decide on a guru
I am turning thirty

And don't have a guru!
no running water flush toilet garbage disposal
and I'm no good at astral projection
can't sleep on a spiked bed
still can't drive stick shift
get pimples once in awhile
and the roof always needs fixing
I am turning thirty

And can't roll a joint
still don't know when to take the bread out
rather have flapjacks and bacon with Vermont maple syrup
or crepes suzette soused in lemon walnut yogurt and honey
with sausage and buttermilk instead of
"health food" any ole day
and don't like to fast
except when I'm hitchhiking
I am turning thirty

4

And can't fix my car
still can't draw hands or feet
and my best friends call me the "walking bust"
because I got conjunctivitis
better known as "pink eye"
am turning thirty

No life insurance
no stocks bonds heavyweight titles
varsity letters or books published by Dell
I am not a famous writer
I am not a famous painter
and my wife tells me
I am only "famous" in my own home
I am turning thirty

The cupboards don't shut right
because I made 'em
the nopales don't taste right
because I just cooked 'em
the kids have reached puberty at the ages of 3 and 4
they are putting me down because I get angry restless impatient
and am "highly spiritual" only at the right times
I am turning thirty

Trying harder every day
to match what I think I am up to the "real" me
I am turning thirty
thirty is turning me, I am up to my neck
in the cosmic wheel
in the clearing clouds, sunlight
thirty years old
the wife bumping up the dusty road
11 o'clock muffler dragging a late summer night
constellations zooming through my head, kids in bed
cookstove cleared, cats purring
invisible wishful thinkings of wine spilled
over my leg from a warm glass of **Dr. Pepper**
turning thirty

Buddha arises in his shrine
our bare feet tiptoe up into the loft
sky breaks thunder, dog farts
a line storm breathes strokes of light
kerosene lamp quivers
my birthday is here, clothes off
rain stopped moon out coyote howling
pinetrees shaking water through the window
wind blows cat meows baby wakes
fill the bottle dawn light
glimmers early morning
planets sway in celestial haze
have I gone mad!

I am not an astronaut
I am not the first man on the Moon
as my friend Dr. Jomo would say
I have not broken any great records

I am thirty years old
and just plain fully awake
the earth is cosmic
and "my" woman is really her own lady
our bed is mulched with war surplus foam
cool sheets in between our legs
it is fall

Going into winter
going into spring going into summer
another time another place another year
and my birthday suddenly doesn't mean a thing
I am thirty years old
tonight, watching the wheel go round
and building my hearth out of
pyramids of light

The Ambition Bird

ANNE SEXTON

So it has come to this—
insomnia at 3:15 A.M.
the clock tolling its engine

like a frog following
a sundial yet having an electric
seizure at the quarter hour.

The business of words keeps me awake.
I am drinking cocoa,
that warm brown mama.

I would like a simple life
yet all night I am laying
poems away in a long box.

It is my immortality box,
my lay-away plan,
my coffin.

All night dark wings
flopping in my heart.
Each an ambition bird.

The bird wants to be dropped
from a high place like Tallahatchie Bridge.

He wants to light a kitchen match
and immolate himself.

He wants to fly into the hand of Michelangelo
and come out painted on a ceiling.

He wants to pierce the hornet's nest
and come out with a long godhead.

He wants to take bread and wine
and bring forth a man happily floating in the Caribbean.

He wants to be pressed out like a key
so he can unlock the Magi.

He wants to take leave among strangers
passing out bits of his heart like hors d'oeuvres.

He wants to die changing his clothes
and bolt for the sun like a diamond.

He wants, I want.
Dear God, wouldn't it be
good enough to just drink cocoa?

I must get a new bird
and a new immortality box.
There is folly enough inside this one.

These Damned Trees Crouch
For W. D. Snodgrass

JIM BARNES

These damned trees crouch heavy under heaven.
As *I* crouch, if I talk, I often cuss
This confounded wood and my own soft heart.
Some hunters like this place and rise at seven
And stand in ease in weather like a lush;
Jim Barnes is crawling through the underbrush.

I don't know why I cannot find *my* house.
It ought to be around here somewhere. Fuss
And bother: the crooked tree, the skunk's art
Lingering on till dark to then arouse
All sleeping demons of the mighty bush;
Jim Barnes is crawling through the underbrush.

My name is just as common as a worm,
And derivative. If I could converse just
With something inside myself and know it
(Have a tête-à-tête with some small gentle germ),
I'd make a beeline home—that's where it starts.
Yes . . . most of all I'd like to be a poet.
But the wood is thick and won't allow old Herm
To come right winging down. I have to rush.
I have to find my house even though it hurts;
Jim Barnes is crawling through the underbrush.

Good Morning, Love!

PAUL BLACKBURN

Rise at 7:15
study the
artifacts
        (2 books
        1 photo
        1 gouache sketch
        2 unclean socks
perform the neces-
sary ablutions
            hands
        face, feet
            crotch
even answer the door
with good grace, even
if it's the light-and-gas man
announcing himself as "EDISON!
Readjer meter, mister?"
For Chrissake yes
        read my meter
        Nothing can alter the euphoria
The blister is still on one finger
        There just are
some mornings worth getting up
& making a cup
of coffee,
            that's all

This Morning
(For the Girls of Eastern High School)

LUCILLE CLIFTON

this morning
this morning
         i met myself
coming in

a bright
jungle girl
shining
quick as a snake
a tall
tree girl a
me girl
         i met myself
this morning
coming in

and all day
i have been
a black bell
ringing
i survive
        survive
survive

My Nurse

STEPHEN SHU NING LIU

It all happened like this:
a young woman came sitting at our door,
I cried and threw myself into the arms
of that woman, shabby, smelly, with an
empty rice bowl in her hand.

So she walked me to the underbrush
where blackberries fantastically grew,
so she wove me a silver crown
of jasmine blossoms in June,
so she made me a good hunter of
grasshoppers in the hay and sat me
tête-à-tête with a jewel-eyed toad,
so she told me about wood elves,
and nightly she sang me to sleep
with her anything-but-music tune.

When she married Wang, a farmer,
firecrackers were banging on the floor,
country folks drank and buzzed,
with their faces ruddy with wine,
and around that blushing couple,
those villagers cracked a dozen
crazy jokes, a lot of baloney.

The Wangs' farm stood by the cornfield,
where a black-and-white dog awoke, barking,
whenever we passed by their bamboo fences
on our fishing trips down the river;
my nurse would come running, calling me,
and stuffing my pocket with melon seeds.

Thus unwittingly I had spent many years
with a she-beggar in those blue-waved hills,
where I glided on like a stream in spring,
where I thrived like snow-peas, all green.
I would never be happier or wiser,
had I had the pleasure to live with a queen.

WILLIAM PITT ROOT

I
I have been the planner
planned by another

far from me, far,
and me no longer:

The earth around me
turns within my mind

to salt. Its unspeakable
savors arrest me.

Looking backward, forward,
thinking, "There is no difference

between them—the present is
never with me."

Anchor me in this earth
that I may live,

whoever loves me!

II
Moving, I love moving
through space

but time appalls me.
I grow dim, fade.

Praise God life's not
a highwire act: I am a bear

as clumsy off the ground
as I am strong among trees.

III
Look backward, look forward,
what is there to see?

I lived once with my own fears
and my wife's

and I moved on. Moved on
but stopped

for one look back,
and froze.

Break me, for godsake
break me down!

Anger me with love now,
and not with caution. Charity

is such a murder. Don't hang
back from me.

IV
I have lived waiting for the blade
to fall.

I could not hide.
The blade was in myself.

Blade was myself.
Self fell: what bonds were cut?

What, whole and shining with strength,
will stride now from its prison

out into eternity?

v
Here there are roses,
planted and tended

by the hands of men.
Berries in the hedges

cluster bright and red.
This is a new year.

I am a new man.
These are new tears.

A Crust of Bread

ALFRED STARR HAMILTON

why, I often wondered
why I was a poet,
first of all

most of all, I wanted
to have been a bird
if I could have been a bird

but I wanted the starlings
to have been fed,
first of all

Sawing the Wood
To Russ & Susan

ARAM SAROYAN

Sawing the wood
So I could be doing something
While just being alive

Sawing the wood
I feel a bird brush by
On the air above my hair

Sawing the wood
So I can think without
Going crazy

Sawing the wood
Because it's good
For my soul

Sawing the wood
Because I'm an ordinary man
In an ordinary world

Sawing the wood
Because my body and my mind
Are one

Sawing the wood
So my blood can move
So my blood can move

Sawing the wood
So I could understand
The nature of time

Sawing the wood
Because unsawed
It won't fit the stove

Sawing the wood
So I can remember
Everybody

Sawing the wood
In order to be
A big success

Sawing the wood
So I will have something
To teach my children

Sawing the wood
So I can be
Completely myself

Sawing the wood
Because I am thirty
Years old

Sawing the wood
To make politics
Ridiculous

Sawing the wood
To make me
Resilient

Sawing the wood
Because two is better
Than one

Sawing the wood
Because the gas
Is almost gone

Sawing the wood
Because life is but a dream
And I am alive

Sawing the wood
Because I'd rather be thin
Than famous

Sawing the wood
Because it is the only good cause
I know

Sawing the wood
Because it keeps my demons
At bay

Sawing the wood
To keep contact
With the saw

Sawing the wood
To know what the fire
Comes from

Sawing the wood
Because it is as good
As music

Sawing the wood
Because I aspire
I aspire

Sawing the wood
Sawing the wood
Sawing the wood

Sawing the wood
Because something tells me
To do it

Sawing the wood
To be alone
With everything

Sawing the wood
To feel the sun
On things

Sawing the wood
Because life is short
And life is long

Sawing the wood
To see the forget-me-nots
When I raise my head

Sawing the wood
To make good
Even better

Sawing the wood
To give the beat
A meaning

Sawing the wood
Because in an hour
It will be dark

Sawing the wood
Because my daughter comes out
To talk to me

Sawing the wood
Because nothing
Is so fulfilling

Sawing the wood
To get behind
The headlines

Sawing the wood
To be a little tired
After awhile

Sawing the wood
To grow old
And wise

Sawing the wood
To make one thing
Into another

Sawing the wood
To get to the bottom
Of the pile

Sawing the wood
Because once I was a boy
And now I am a man

Sawing the wood
Because my father
Is older than me

Sawing the wood
Because my mother
Is older than me

Sawing the wood
Because my wife
Is inside sewing

Projected View of 2000

FREYA MANFRED

I will be an old woman in a red cotton dress riding a bicycle.
Behind me I will tie two wicker baskets filled with tulips,
ducks and quick dogs, a small garden quacking and panting
behind me.

I will wear rouge made of cherries on my cheeks and a yellow
sunflower on a garter snake chain around my neck.

I will eat seeds and peach pits and celery hearts and drink
elderberry wine in stables full of straw and cobwebs.

I will scratch the cow's back and the horse's ear and sing
off-key to them, "Bringing in the Sheaves," and "Mint Julep."

I will carry a pearl-handled revolver in my cardigan sweater
pocket, loaded with sunflower seeds.

I will tell more huge purple lies than thin white truths, so
people who have small eyes will open them wider.

I will campaign for the man who has the darkest and softest
beard for president, or else I will marry him.

I will grow as many wrinkles on my body as I possibly can,
and I will throw my two floppy wrinkled breasts over one
shoulder when I play basketball.

I will live in a house made of stained-glass church windows.

I will put oysters and amber spiked bon-bons in small goblets on the cemetery gravestones.

I will pick my nose in company, and I will play the fiddle.

When I die, the gnome and the elf from Norway will make me into small leather shoes and little leather aprons for the children of a nearby mushroom dealer.

In Those Times

ALLAN BLOCK

The air was lilac and lavender.
Sticks and stones, mud and water

fell into cities under my hand.
Mother gasped and Father learned

he'd got a jewel. My balsa plane
won the derby for good design.

A fiddle tucked under my chin
brought down the auditorium.

My whittled baits caught pickerel
where no pickerel swam, still

I shaped nothing until brute
language came and drove me to it.

Foibles

HAROLD BOND

I: HP

You were always a one to
call a spade a petunia.
Your forbidding tongue lashed at
our vernacular, that the
iron lungs we tenanted

were not sardine cans: they were
"respirators." You saddled
the wrack of our bodies with
exercises, heat treatments.
Behind your back we called you

amazon. You envied us.
You told us the afflicted
are assured a place in the
hereafter. It was vaguely
Biblical, like clear water

over stone. Would you have thought
my laundryman years later
would label my shirts with an
"HP"? Or that the state of
Massachusetts, year after

year, would issue my license
plates with an HP also?
It was right somehow, neither
a euphemism nor a
fish can: handicapped person.

You would envy me my glib
identification, my
clear waters flowing to the
hereafter. For you I would
sell my car and go shirtless.

II: Acquaintances

Grocer, tailor, all my stock
acquaintances, behind your
elastic smiles there is the
assumption I am less than
intelligent. You watch me.

You equate my clumsy walk,
my paralytic hands with
my intelligence. And I
disappoint you. Always there
is the expectation I

will drool or make guttural
sounds or have convulsions. I
can do all three but I will
not let you see me with my
hair down in public. I will

remain articulate and
deep-throated and immensely
ethereal. Yet I am
grateful for your improbable
amenities. I am "sir"

to you despite your knowledge
of my madness. You ask me
for the weather. You smile when
I tell you it is snowing
in July. I will sustain

your fable. I will have you
all in my home. I will squat
for you. I will scratch my arm
pits and grunt like an ape. And
you will say, Thank you. Thank you.

III: The Game

You are my friends. You do things
for me. My affliction is
your hangup. It is yours more
than it ever could be mine.
You spread my affliction thin

enough to go around once
for all of us. You put my
coat on for me when I ask
you. You put my coat on for
me when I do not ask you.

You embrace my shoes with your
compassion. You tell me I
would be less apt to fall with
rubber soles. You carry things
for me. You tell me they are

heavy things. How it would be
difficult for anyone
to carry them. You open
mustard bottles for me. You
tell me how hard it is to

open mustard bottles. I
agree with you. I will not
destroy our game. At night I
dream I am Samson. I will
topple coliseums. I

will overwhelm you with my
brute power. I will knock you
dead. I will open mustard
bottles for you. I will show
you how easy it really is.

Legacies and Bastard Roses
(to mom and mamacita)

ALMA VILLANUEVA

I thought of you last night
after
I washed my face, my skin
is dry now so
I add oil to soften it or
I crack and
I remember you applying
and reapplying oils
to your face and neck, you
always told me
a girl could never be
too careful.

(mom)

don't forget. men come
and go. your friends

stay. women
stay. I
heard this at 7
and never forgot.

(mom)

he raped me
and I never told
anyone,
not even *mi*
mama, I
was so ashamed, I
lay in the tub
for hours
emptying
the tub and
refilling
it, crying
softly.
my tears fell
softly,
into the
dirty
water.

(mom)

he passed me on the road
that day in Louisiana
that day I walked all
the way to town
carrying you
carrying a suitcase
in the heat
that day
he passed
that uppity Mexican
that day

(mom)

my family
always
said, 'marry a good mexican
boy'—
        but the sun on a
gringo's hair makes me
worship
them

(mamacita)

when a man opens a woman, she
is like a rose, she
will never close
again.

ever.

(me)

pistils. stamens.
wavering in the sun.
a bloom on the bush.
a mixed bloom.
they wonder at it.
a bastard rose.
a wild rose.
colors gone mad.
a rupture of thorns.
you must not pluck it.
you must recognize
    a magic rose
                    when
you see it.

For My Father

PHILIP WHALEN

Being a modest man, you wanted
Expected an ordinary child
And here's this large, inscrutable object

                ME

        (Buddha's mother only dreamed
                of a white elephant;
            my mother . . .)

Cross between a TV camera and a rotary press
Busy turning itself into many printed pages
Heavy, a dust-collector, almost impossible
                to get off your hands, out of your house
Whatever it was, not an actual child

You recognize parts of the works, ones you first donated
But what are they doing—the flywheel horizontal
Spinning two directions at once
A walking-beam connected to a gear train turning camshafts—
Which produces material like this
Sometimes worth money to folks in New York
Or not, nobody knows why.

A True Account of Talking to the Sun at Fire Island

FRANK O'HARA

The Sun woke me this morning loud
and clear, saying "Hey! I've been
trying to wake you up for fifteen
minutes. Don't be so rude, you are
only the second poet I've ever chosen
to speak to personally
so why
aren't you more attentive? If I could
burn you through the window I would
to wake you up. I can't hang around
here all day."
"Sorry, Sun, I stayed
up late last night talking to Hal."

"When I woke up Mayakovsky he was
a lot more prompt" the Sun said
petulantly. "Most people are up
already waiting to see if I'm going
to put in an appearance."
I tried
to apologize "I missed you yesterday."
"That's better" he said. "I didn't
know you'd come out." "You may be
wondering why I've come so close?"
"Yes" I said beginning to feel hot
wondering if maybe he wasn't burning me
anyway.

"Frankly I wanted to tell you
I like your poetry. I see a lot
on my rounds and you're okay. You may
not be the greatest thing on earth, but
you're different. Now, I've heard some
say you're crazy, they being excessively
calm themselves to my mind, and other
crazy poets think that you're a boring
reactionary. Not me.
                          Just keep on
like I do and pay no attention. You'll
find that people always will complain
about the atmosphere, either too hot
or too cold too bright or too dark, days
too short or too long.
                          If you don't appear
at all one day they think you're lazy
or dead. Just keep right on, I like it.

And don't worry about your lineage
poetic or natural. The Sun shines on
the jungle, you know, on the tundra
the sea, the ghetto. Wherever you were
I knew it and saw you moving. I was waiting
for you to get to work.

                          And now that you
are making your own days, so to speak,
even if no one reads you but me
you won't be depressed. Not
everyone can look up, even at me. It
hurts their eyes."
                          "Oh Sun, I'm so grateful to you!"

"Thanks and remember I'm watching. It's
easier for me to speak to you out
here. I don't have to slide down
between buildings to get your ear.
I know you love Manhattan, but
you ought to look up more often.

                    And
always embrace things, people earth
sky stars, as I do, freely and with
the appropriate sense of space. That
is your inclination, known in the heavens
and you should follow it to hell, if
necessary, which I doubt.

                    Maybe we'll
speak again in Africa, of which I too
am specially fond. Go back to sleep now
Frank, and I may leave a tiny poem
in that brain of yours as my farewell."

"Sun, don't go!" I was awake
at last. "No, go I must, they're calling
me."
     "Who are they?"
                   Rising he said "Some
day you'll know. They're calling to you
too." Darkly he rose, and then I slept.

April Inventory

W. D. SNODGRASS

The green catalpa tree has turned
All white; the cherry blooms once more.
In one whole year I haven't learned
A blessed thing they pay you for.
The blossoms snow down in my hair;
The trees and I will soon be bare.

The trees have more than I to spare.
The sleek, expensive girls I teach,
Younger and pinker every year,
Bloom gradually out of reach.
The pear tree lets its petals drop
Like dandruff on a tabletop.

The girls have grown so young by now
I have to nudge myself to stare.
This year they smile and mind me how
My teeth are falling with my hair.
In thirty years I may not get
Younger, shrewder, or out of debt.

The tenth time, just a year ago,
I made myself a little list
Of all the things I'd ought to know,
Then told my parents, analyst,
And everyone who's trusted me
I'd be substantial, presently.

I haven't read one book about
A book or memorized one plot.
Or found a mind I did not doubt.

I learned one date. And then forgot.
And one by one the solid scholars
Get the degrees, the jobs, the dollars.

And smile above their starchy collars.
I taught my classes Whitehead's notions;
One lovely girl, a song of Mahler's.
Lacking a source-book or promotions,
I showed one child the colors of
A luna moth and how to love.

I taught myself to name my name,
To bark back, loosen love and crying;
To ease my woman so she came,
To ease an old man who was dying.
I have not learned how often I
Can win, can love, but choose to die.

I have not learned there is a lie
Love shall be blonder, slimmer, younger;
That my equivocating eye
Loves only by my body's hunger;
That I have forces, true to feel,
Or that the lovely world is real.

While scholars speak authority
And wear their ulcers on their sleeves,
My eyes in spectacles shall see
These trees procure and spend their leaves.
There is a value underneath
The gold and silver in my teeth.

Though trees turn bare and girls turn wives,
We shall afford our costly seasons;
There is a gentleness survives
That will outspeak and has its reasons.
There is a loveliness exists,
Preserves us, not for specialists.

The Legacy

MARGE PIERCY

Bury that family grandeur
of mink in mothballs,
rotting marble. Stop
lugging through furnished rooms
ancestral portraits
in a deck of marked cards.
Toss out those wroughtiron crutches.
Success like an incubus
visits your bed.
Nothing you do
will ever be enough.
You cannot win a prize
grand enough to ransom
your mother's youth.
The incense of those years
one by one guttered out
faint light, faint heat
chokes me in your room,
smothers you as you sleep
dreaming in hand-me-downs,
while dead women's wishes
like withered confetti
snow through your head.

Dickey in Tucson

R. P. DICKEY

The Catalina mountains romp, saddled with snow,
dappled like an Appaloosa stallion,
while down here in the foothills where I live
the thermometer climbs to Gabriel Fahrenheit 77.

On the desert floor: saguaro, soaptree yucca,
cholla, prickly pear, mesquite, palo verde:
each stands its own   discrete   ground
in a pattern of harmonious disunity.

I look and this dramatic earth subtles
into my arteries, flushes out into my muscles.
I'm not a painter, but if I were
I'd love this light even more than I do now.

Just over a stone's throw away, neighbors
keep Palominos in small corrals. February, and
I put out my first-ever vegetable garden,
sequestered from the drunken sting of cacti.

My son Ez rides Silver, his creosote stick horse,
all over two wild acres of kitty litter;
my wife patches up my clothes, edits a cookbook,
sells insurance, writes stuff better than mine.

(Molly Bloom, our border collie, stays happy
all the time. The four solid black cats
keep us from too much bad luck, ill health,
too many steep bills, setbacks, letdowns, cutoffs.)

In a house full of books and no TV
I snack around the clock, rummage dumbly
for meanings, listen to a little recorded Bach,
take lots of notes, dance with my main cat, Neffy.

I go out to Mass, jog, take a hike with Ez
(telling him what I've just read about barrel cactus),
or on the stoop read a pedantic book on Pima shamanism,
sprinkle the garden, lift weights, loaf in a green swimsuit.

This is southern Arizona, middle of winter,
talking to me. This is where I live.
I came here for what ails me;
and, cowboy, I aim to stay a while.

The Diet

SUSAN MERNIT

I am the child fat and contented,
the daughter sweet and obese.
oh please grow fatter my dear little girl
ten pounds more and I'll eat you up.
Clothing binds me.   an envelope of promise,
a cylinder of lard, I am the chuckle of a
candy bar.
3 times a day, once after school, before
bed or dinner and with cigarettes
I remove my clothes and eat like the moon.
I am the man in command.

BREAD   LETTUCE   APPLES   CHEESE
    SODA CRACKERS   TEA
After supper I take a snack and bring my mother beer.

You'll be gorgeous when you're thin
would you like a yellow bathing suit ?
I am a milkmaid in the sun, I cache candy in my hand.
Christmas, Thanksgiving, Easter, Spring
I break bread with myself, served wherever I am.
My very stretch is a rippling stroll
I am a turkey in heat.

I like to be fat when I take a man.   he cannot
want me for myself alone.   body hated and overcome
raped by him, I am left untouched.
do I tire of eating?   No.

I see a fat girl beside a spring.   Her lunch
is done, she is reading a book.
the trees and breezes pull and waft   the elk
and deer bow
Calling to her is a unicorn
who sees a virgin, thin.

My Mother

ROBERT MEZEY

My mother writes from Trenton,
a comedian to the bone
but underneath serious
and all heart. 'Honey,' she says,
'be a mensch and Mary too,
its no good, to worry, you
are doing the best you can
your Dad and everyone
thinks you turned out very well
as long as you pay your bills
nobody can say a word
you can tell them to drop dead
so save a dollar it can't
hurt—remember Frank you went
to highschool with? he still lives
with his wife's mother, his wife
works while he writes his books and
did he ever sell a one
the four kids run around naked
36, and he's never had,
you'll forgive my expression
even a pot to piss in
or a window to throw it,

such a smart boy he couldnt
read the footprints on the wall
honey you think you know all
the answers you dont, please, try
to put some money away
believe me it wouldn't hurt
artist shmartist life's too short
for that kind of, forgive me,
horseshit, I know what you want
better than you, all that counts
is to make a good living
and the best of everything,
as Sholem Aleichem said,
he was a great writer did
you ever read his books dear,
you should make what he makes a year
anyway he says some place
Poverty is no disgrace
but its no honor either
that's what I say,
                    love,
                        Mother'

The Day of the Dead

D. W. DONZELLA

On this day in Sicily
the children receive gifts
in the names of the dead of their families.
Better ones than on Christmas.

I have been given these names:
Poidomani, Camillieri, Lissandrello, Donzella.
I have something of their faces, hands and ways.
I know how they arrived here
and why they stayed.

Mostly I know their vendettas.
I have many cousins I was not permitted to know
for the animosity between these dead.
Words spoken after wine have lasted as long
as the mummies of loved ones some families keep
in Palermo's catacombs.

My family does not know itself.
It is scattered like a brain struck by a bullet
with a cross cut into its tip.
It does not understand itself
nor does it ever forget.
It meets at funerals with great concern
and treats the living with neglect.

The monks at the catacombs used to stuff the dead
and stand them up in rows, fully dressed,
to be visited, spoken with,
consulted on family matters
in the presence of children.

These dead stand there yet,
hunched and bent by responsibility.

They wait in the dark to be asked.

Beginnings and Endings

PHYLLIS KOESTENBAUM

That child in the picture on my mother's dresser-top
is my child not me   in another picture I lean
against my brother Shelley   my dress is nearly white
shantung they called it   there is eyelet above my breasts
I sewed badly   the teacher let Aunt Pearlie finish
it on her machine   I traveled on the BMT
with Elise Gruber   she owned fifteen matched sweater sets
we looked up menstruation in the dictionary
we said our parents wouldn't do it
I wore it to graduation   Mrs. Vanderpool
held my hand in hers   I cried   I felt like throwing up
she said I was beautiful   we do not smile   my rose
corsage droops   we wear glasses   I don't look beautiful
I am ready to say good-bye   I begin again
it is time   my hair is gray like hers

I will not accuse them any more   in that fading
picture my eyes charge you didn't love me   not enough
you loved him more   you always loved him more   the rag man
called old clothes cash   I could be the rag man   they're asleep
as I was in my coffin of a bed   old clothes cash
the sun is always out when the rag man comes   Shelley
where is Shelley   is he asleep too in his twin bed
once a lady asked if we were twins   I couldn't say
good-bye then   Shelley left for Harvard   I was alone
with them   I went to Daddy's school   I had a red purse
I didn't wear lipstick   Daddy said lipstick was cheap
Elise Gruber went to Madison   Judy Reisner
went to Madison   I was alone with them   Carol
Leventhal went to Madison   Mother said you must
listen to Daddy he knows best   I dreamed of Shelley

I begged Shelley to rescue me   Shelley was away
at Harvard   when he came home for Thanksgiving I dreamed
again and called out loud from my foyer cot Shelley
save me   Harry Mendelssohn came home with him   Harry
said he'd like to get me drunk—Shelley played me Handel
he gave me books to read   Dos Passos   Romain Rolland

It is time   Mother is frail in my arms   she covers
her cancer scars with cream   she plucks her eyebrows   she lines
her eyelids with pencil and colors her cheeks with rouge
the children call her hair cotton candy   she tells me
her diamond rings are mine   I tell her I don't need them
I look in my mirror and see her face   Daddy wears
a cap   it is harder to say good-bye to Daddy
he averts his eyes   he will not look at me   brown brown
eyes   my eyes   the eyes of his rabbi father   zayda
you never kissed me zayda   but I smelled you in our
house   did you kiss Shelley since he was a boy   you taught
him Talmud on a bridge table in the living room
I brought you a pear on a glass plate with a paring
knife   I still smell you zayda   when you died no one cried
we ate applesauce at the table   Daddy was gone
I cry today for your death   Daddy put your picture
in the hallway in a dark place   I do not find love
in your eyes   your beard is marvelous   their house could be
a tunnel   in a brighter place they have hung an oil
painting they found in London of a rabbi reading
the light enters from above   I do not say good-bye
to that holiness   I say good-bye to bitterness
to expectations that sit like dust in tight corners

Where have they put my wedding pictures
maybe up in the closet with my wedding dress wrapped
in cellophane   Mother dyed her dress
green   Mother was a beautiful bride
in one I am fragile as snow   the photographer
was one of Daddy's students   in another I laugh
like a good child   I tried to say good-bye   it was time

there is a smudge on my bare shoulder   my hair is wild
Grandma's hair is cut in a boy's bob   pearls wind around
her thin throat   it is her last picture   her eyes are small
I smile in all my childhood pictures except one   there
I wear a blue sailor's coat with a big white collar
I have ribbons in my hair   why don't I smile   I hold
a doll by its head   we are linked with our brown brown eyes

I trail scars the way young pretty girls hang their long clean
hair   Mother do you remember how I combed your hair
long hours in the red chair with chocolates beside you
the knick-knacks clean in the lamplight   Daddy smoked his pipe
I hugged you in the kitchen   I said I love you love
you   it is time   Josh tries to say good-bye and can't   Josh
you said he is beautiful a beautiful baby
and a boy   do you remember how I combed your hair
where was Shelley   I wake in that hospital room   bars
on the bed   but I am not an animal   wake up
wake up   I said good-bye then   a three-week clot of cells
is not a baby   Daddy I write like you   I burn
with poetry   Daddy did you think
I would write poetry   I begin
with my poetry   that child in the picture is my
child not me

Identities

AL YOUNG

So youre playing
Macbeth in Singapore
1937 before you were
even born perhaps

The lady is warm,
your lines are waiting
in your stomach
to be heard.

An old seacoast drunk
in pullover blue cap
stomps up one-legged
onto the stage to
tell you youve got no
business playing this
bloody Macbeth,
not a lonely black boy
like you, lost like
himself in a new world
where it's no longer
a matter of whom
thou knowest so much
as it is who you know.
(Say the lady warming
is a career bohemian
with OK looks & a
Vassar education)

Say the future seems
fractured in view of
the worsening wars
in Europe & Asia &
the old man's just
shattered your last
chance illusion.

Well, do you go on
& Shakespeare anyway
or reach for the sky
for the 500th time?

The Bagley Iowa Poem

ANN DARR

1.
Bagley meant to be
a railroad town
but the railroad
hadn't heard.

Three churches
poulticed
600 people.
(five ninety-nine
after I ran away.)

The sneaky holy-roller summer—
with Christian Endeavor
serving as the dating bureau—
on Main street sat the Methodist madam.

God's sparrow
never flew in our trees
and the angling birch
filling my window
turned into a creaking skeleton
when I became
homesick at home.

2.
No was a great big
thousand letter word
and the consequences
were plenty.

Yes was love
and all that
meant, soured
and scourged
with unhappy knots
that tied the men
to their women
and the women
to their men
and the land
heaved and buckled
and produced
2¢ a bushel
    corn
and separate rooms.

3.
Bagley,
well, yes,
heaved on winter streets,
sweltered in the summer.
Grandma Plummer,
deaf as a post
hole,
traded the attic
for a double-carpeted
dining room
two husbands later.
I don't think I
was through with weddings
before I began but
the illustrations
were out of focus
and the hills
were full of accidents
and proposals.

4.

I fly back to my childhood
trying to get the water-tower
shape right. Shaped like a—

I sneak up on it through the trees,
the apple trees that are young
and shapely. Shaped like—

There on its long spindly legs,
the fat tub of a water-tower
towers over the splattered town

shaped like a great bruise
with the welts running like
mainstreet and over it the water tower

shaped like a Roman candle
waiting to go off if only
someone would set a match to it.

I bring my torch. Water
tower shaped like Canaveral.
Over and over I have dreamed
of seeing Bagley from the moon.

5.

Learning that the town has no more trains or buses
shouldn't matter to me who will never go there again but
it has put me standing on a corner
under the bus stop sign
in my new graduation suit
and a hat with a flowing scarf
of a color I can't remember
but the dust is blowing—
gum wrappers mince down the street
making their small journey—
and I am headed away.

Letter to Donald Fall

ALAN DUGAN

I walked a hangover like my death down
the stairs from the shop and opened the door
to a spring snow sticking only to the tops
of air-conditioners and convertibles, and thought
of my friend Donald Fall in San Francisco.
Toothless in spring!, old friend, I count
my other blessings after friendship
unencumbered by communion: I have:
a money-making job, time off it, a wife
I still love sometimes unapproachably
hammering on picture frames, my own
city that I wake to, that the snow
has come to noiselessly at night, it's there
by morning, swallowing the sounds of spring
and traffic, and my new false teeth,
shining and raw in the technician's lab
like Grails, saying, "We are the resurrection
and the life: tear out the green stumps
of your aching and put plastic on instead:
immortality is in science and machines."
I, as an aging phony, stale, woozy, and corrupt
from unattempted dreams and bad health habits,
am comforted: the skunk cabbage generates its
frost-thawing fart-gas in New Jersey and the first
crocuses appear in Rockefeller Center's Channel Gardens:
Fall, it is not so bad at Dugan's Edge.

Verses *Versus* Verses

MARVIN BELL

First, there's the courtship
and that's seven poems,
and the marriage costs three,
and then comes the first birth
which costs more than just several,
although succeeding births
grow less expensive, but more
routine, but then there's the
children's schooling, which
costs two decades and three or four
hundred and thirty seven
poems, with some interest,
and you worry about borrowing, until,
one night at dinner, there's the
possibility of retirement,
and you have them disconnect
the utilities, and there
go four poems—gas, oil,
water and electricity—and
a good meal in a restaurant
by this time costs one hundred
lines with a sonnet for the tip,
but you wouldn't have it any
other way, and you *wouldn't* have it
any other way, so you're held up
and when you sell out, you throw in
six thieves and a title
for good measure.

Rosemary

ROSEMARY DANIELL

Rosemary.
  Rosemary Hughes.
        Rosemary Hughes Ramos
      Rosemary Hughes Ramos Daniell
Rosemary Hughes Ramos Daniell Coppelman.
    Rosemary Hughes Ramos Daniell
        Rosemary Hughes Ramos
      Rosemary Hughes
Rosemary who's?
  Rosemary's.

Jamming with the Band at the VFW

DAVID BOTTOMS

I played old Country and Western
then sat alone at a table near the bandstand,
smug in the purple light that seemed like a bruised sun
going down over Roswell, Georgia.

A short bald man in a black string tie
and a woman with a red beehive
waltzed across the floor
like something out of Lawrence Welk,
his hips moving like a metronome in baggy pants,
hers following like a mirror image.

For a long time I watched and drank beer,
listened to the tear-jerking music,
thought of all my written words,
all the English classes, the workshops,
the MA stored safely under my cowboy hat,
the arty sophisticates and educated queers
who attend poetry readings in Atlanta

and weighed against them
not one bald man waltzing a woman through another Blitz,
but all men turning gray who dream of having died
at Anzio, Midway, Guadalcanal.

Then rising from my chair
I drank the last of the Pabst
and moved through the bruised light of the bandstand
onto the purple dance floor, toward the tables
across the room, toward the table beside the bar,
and there the woman with platinum hair
and rhinestone earrings, moving suddenly toward me.

Not at All What One Is Used To . . .

ISABELLA GARDNER

There was never any worry about bread or even butter
although that worried me almost as much as my stutter.
I drank coffee with the others in drugstores and then went
back to my room for which I paid a lower rent
than I could afford and where I was proud
of the bedbugs, and where I often allowed
myself an inadequate little Rhine wine. Two
or three times a week after seeing the producers who
were said to be looking for comedy types I wandered
off to the movies alone and always wondered
if anyone in the mezzanine knew me by sight, or might
know me by name or have kissed me and I felt an itch
to stand right up and ask, like swearing out loud in church.
Only one agent agreed to be rude to me every day, a
cross cockeyed woman who had acted in her youth.
I was not union because I had never been paid and the truth
is no other agent would speak to me or even see me until I was
     Equity . . .
a vicious circle but not unpleasing to me.
I smoked for hours in producers' anterooms where
I prayed that interviews I had come there
to beseech would be denied.
Usually my prayers were granted and I stayed outside.
I was a tense impostor, a deliberate dunce,
in a lobby of honest earnest seekers. Once
or twice thanks to a letter of introduction I
got to see the man, but instead of "chin up" and "do or die"
I effectively slouched and stammered in disorder in order
to thus escape the chance to read I might be
offered. An English director once said I was the
"perfect adorable silly ass," due in part to a part

he saw me do in which I had to lisp and giggle.
But that of course was in another country. I did not boggle
at summer stock and somewhere north of Boston I had
at last become a paid member of a company where sad
to relate I was successfully grotesque in numerous unglamorous
bit parts (usually dialect for I did not stutter
in dialect) and I was always differently grotesque, utter-
ly; but people laughed and/or cried, always saying I was playing myself, that I was a "natural." Through the good offices of a
well-connected friend I at last read for a producer who was
      Broadway
and was given the part of a Cockney maid, afraid
and eager, who moved and talked in double-time.
But I was fired. The stars complained for no rime
or reason that they became confused when I was "on" (there
      was no basis
for their saying that the audience laughed too much and in the
      wrong places)
although it is possible that I just did everything faster and faster
I had come to depend on the laughs and dismissal was a disaster.
My next job was a haughty lady's maid with a faint brogue
and a strip-tease walk. One night (in Hartford) I was more
      rogue-
ish than usual and the college boys broke up the show
banging their feet on the floor and whistling. Not long ago
I portrayed a madwoman (but gentle and sentimental)
I curtseyed, sang a short song as I did not
stammer when I sang, and fondled a telescope that
had belonged to a sea-going ancestor. It was agreed
that at last, despite previous successes, I had indeed
and finally found my niche. It was declared
that I could go on and on doing that kind of thing, but I dared
myself to attempt only straight parts although it is hard (playing
      with fire)
for a character actress to play herself and only too true
that the audience response is not at all what one is used to.
Nevertheless it is a challenge and no reason to retire.

Nowata

DAVID RAY

The town needed me.
It drove me on. Winters,
I slid on the iced rails
Of streetcars.
Summers, I dished stew
Down at the Oasis Grill
and Poolhall, another place
The decent folk
Wouldn't want to look
For love or stew or snooker.
Ah, little did rich old Landers
Know how good that stew was,
Called "Mulligan."
The town needed me,
Desperately.
One June I mowed the whole
Cemetery, then swept the stones.
It's a wonder I didn't build that town.
But I return, and there's still
No town built there
Nor anyone sowing the seeds
Of *Communitas*
On the right side of the tracks.
But I cross over and stare
Where chickens peck
At the ruins of black Myrtle's shack.

Unwanted

EDWARD FIELD

The poster with my picture on it
Is hanging on the bulletin board in the Post Office.

I stand by it hoping to be recognized
Posing first full face and then profile

But everybody passes by and I have to admit
The photograph was taken some years ago.

I was unwanted then and I'm unwanted now
Ah guess ah'll go up echo mountain and crah.

I wish someone would find my fingerprints somewhere
Maybe on a corpse and say, You're it.

Description: Male, or reasonably so
White, but not lily-white and usually deep-red

Thirty-fivish, and looks it lately
Five-feet-nine and one-hundred-thirty pounds: no physique

Black hair going gray, hairline receding fast
What used to be curly, now fuzzy

Brown eyes starey under beetling brow
Mole on chin, probably will become a wen

It is perfectly obvious that he was not popular at school
No good at baseball, and wet his bed.

His aliases tell his history: Dumbbell, Good-for-nothing,
Jewboy, Fieldinsky, Skinny, Fierce Face, Greaseball, Sissy.

Warning: This man is not dangerous, answers to any name
Responds to love, don't call him or he will come.

In Sympathy, but Only for a Little Longer

ANN MENEBROKER

everyone's
doing their job
but annie
and she can't
because she doesn't
feel up to it
and gets claustrophobia
she's thirsty
she has to go wee wee
she's tired
she's horny
she can't face people
without slipping into them
like a toe checking
water temperature
she feels unsafe
she drinks and gets sick
she sweats easily
she doesn't like her face
she needs to be alone
97% of the time
we keep telling annie
we understand
because we want her to feel
loved
and we hope she gets well soon
because she is
a pain in the ass

Fresh Meat

It was Thanksgiving.
The men were watching the ball game.
They were passing around the new Remington,
running their hands up and down the barrel,
throwing it to their shoulders, getting doubles.

I stood in the kitchen where I came to everyone's
breasts. I liked it there. I liked the heat.
I liked to watch the women bend over and look
in the oven.

"Get your .22," said my father. "We're going
down to the pasture."
"He's too young," my mother said.
My father, "Get your rifle."

Everyone went in two cars. I rode with the women
in a Buick that had idled and warmed. By the
time we got there the men had spread out
across the wide acres belonging to old man Eckart.

My mother and her sisters wore dainty rubber boots
with fur around the ankles. They stepped carefully
as herons. Ahead of us in khaki and Iwo
camouflage stalked my father.

The pasture was not long and ended in a tall
hedgerow. Beyond that, City Route 50 defended by
hamburger stands. Cautious as white hunters
the men prowled and met us coming back.

I was not allowed to carry live ammunition
and asked my father for a shell.
"What for?" said my mother.
He answered, "Here."

I knocked the dirt out of a milk bottle
and asked him to throw it in the air.
"What if he kills someone?" said the women.
The men, "The hell with that let the kid try."

I rubbed the shell free of lint, touched it
to the tip of my tongue. "Why not shoot on
the ground where you can hit it," said my mother.

"Get ready!" my father said. When I nodded
the bottle rose. At its zenith it hesitated
and I blew it to bits.

"Goddamn," said the basses.
I looked at my mother who stood with her hands
buried in her coolie sleeves. I snapped the shell
out of the chamber. I went over and stood
with the men.

Ten Week Wife

RHODA DONOVAN

Dried to a pit of meanness,
talking to nobody, looking

out from the wrong side of my face,
I was a salt flat, a dug

out road bed, six feet of wasp
and a worse sting coming,

a sucked egg, a picked chicken,
a doll wound up and run

down, been everywhere,
done by everybody.

Then you eased in,
squeezed in, thumping

new life, plumping me.
Now I am a Toby jug,

round and sassy, sleek and smooth
and puffed up full of you,

my old frame fleshed out,
sod breaking to bloom,

salt gone sweet, wasp unstung,
a laid egg, a done doll

picked up and planted,
making roots, driving them deep,

growing smug, feeling like
a balloon in a world with no pins.

The Landscape Inside Me

THOMAS MC GRATH

Here I go riding through my morning self
Between West Elbow and Little East Elbow,
Between Hotspur Heart and the Islands of Langerhans,
On the Rock Island Line of my central nervous system.

And I note the landscape which inhabits me—
How excellent in the morning to be populated by trees!
And all the hydrants are manned by dogs
And every dog is a landscape full of fleas,

And every flea is an index to the mountains!
I am well pleased with myself that I've kept the mountains.
What I can't understand is why I've kept the smog,
But since it inhabits me, why should I deny it?

Especially, why deny it on a morning like this
When I've a large unidentified star in my left
Elbow and in my head a windy palette of birds,
And a lively line-storm crossing my pancreas?

My Mother Takes My Wife's Side

DAVID KHERDIAN

This is an
ignominious tale about the naming
of a family of which I am a member.
Our name, I must (reluctantly)
confess, is Turkish, and occurred
so long ago that our true Armenian
name has been lost—perhaps forever.

One early evening, in an unknown year
of our Lord, one of my forefathers—
(a maker of doors;—a carpenter) went
to a Turk's home to collect on the
door he had made him.

The Turk wouldn't be bothered and
slammed the door of the door-
maker into the door-maker's face,
      WHEREUPON,
the carpenter,
enraged in a fury that
is common to Armenians
but as puzzling to *odars*
as their behavior is puzzling to us,
broke the door in two
        and fled.

"Kherda khatchda," the Turk exclaimed, or
kherda (broke), *khatchda* (run).

The name stuck.

And what may seem
a casual incident for the naming of
such a name is not,
for the name couldn't have been more
accurate, or the mood in which the
action took place more fitting,
for the Kherdians have always been,
and are still,
impulsive and crazy—
"a little touched"
we used to say as kids—
An expression that recalls my father.

And this afternoon
in discussing marriages and the faults
of men with my mother, and after she
had denounced every male that we had
moved into the conversation,
I asked with an innocence I enjoy
affecting:

"And what is my fault as a husband?"

"You ask that!" she shouts, "after
storming out of the house yesterday,
leaving your wife with tears in her face!

Your crazy Armenian temper is your fault!
Need it be asked? Must it be told?"

"Kherda khatchda," I say, smiling.

"Pot kut," my mother replies in Turkish,
two words of another meaning
better designed to describe
this particular Kherdian.

A Snapshot of the Auxiliary

RICHARD HUGO

In this photo, circa 1934,
you see the women of the St. James Lutheran
Womens Auxiliary. It is easy
to see they are German, short, squat,
with big noses, the sadness of the Dakotas
in their sullen mouths. These are exceptions:
Mrs. Kyte, English, who hated me.
I hated her and her husband.
Mrs. Noraine, Russian, kind. She saved me once
from a certain whipping. Mrs. Hillborn,
Swedish I think. Cheerful. Her husband
was a cop. None of them seem young. Perhaps
the way the picture was taken. Thinking back
I never recall a young face, a pretty one.
My eyes were like this photo. Old.

This one is Grandmother. This my Aunt Sarah,
still living. That one—I forget her name—
the one with maladjusted sons. That gray
in the photo was actually their faces.
On gray days we reflected weather color.
Lutherans did that. It made us children of God.
That one sang so loud and bad, I blushed.
She believed she believed the words.
She turned me forever off hymns. Even
the good ones, the ones they founded jazz on.

Many of them have gone the way wind recommends
or, if you're religious, God. Mrs. Noraine,
thank the wind, is alive. The church
is brick now, not the drab board frame
you see in the background. Once I was alone
in there and the bells, the bells started to ring.
They terrified me home. This next one in the album
is our annual picnic. We are all having fun.

Marthe, the Mar, la Mer, La Mère, tram, he, rath, mare, hear my mère, my mart . . .

COLETTE INEZ

we never gave each other groceries.
No brown bags with celery tops,
scouts feeling the air with their leaves.
No leaves between us. You left me with the Sisters.
My father was a brother. My father was a father
to the church.

There were many leaves when we were two.
I, in the branch stems of your veins,
I, red flower, the only one
blooming in the courtyard of your womb.
I howled like a freshly cut rose.
They put me in a vase. I grew fragrant in a country
where no one had a nose.

I, too, am not a mother although once
in a house full of roses, father sky, mother breath,
I left my child with the sisters of death.

Writ on the Eve of My 32nd Birthday
A Slow Thoughtful Spontaneous Poem

GREGORY CORSO

I am 32 years old
and finally I look my age, if not more.
Is it a good face what's no more a boy's face?
It seems fatter. And my hair,
it's stopped being curly. Is my nose big?
The lips are the same.
And the eyes, ah the eyes get better all the time.
32 and no wife, no baby; no baby hurts,
  but there's lots of time.
I don't act silly any more.
And because of it I have to hear from so-called friends:
"You've changed. You used to be so crazy so great."
They are not comfortable with me when I'm serious.
Let them go to the Radio City Music Hall.
32; saw all of Europe, met millions of people;
  was great for some, terrible for others.
I remember my 31st year when I cried:
"To think I may have to go another 31 years!"
I don't feel that way this birthday.
I feel I want to be wise with white hair in a tall library
  in a deep chair by a fireplace.
Another year in which I stole nothing.
8 years now and haven't stole a thing!
I stopped stealing!
But I still lie at times,
and still am shameless yet ashamed when it comes
  to asking for money.
32 years old and four hard real funny sad bad wonderful
  books of poetry
—the world owes me a million dollars.

I think I had a pretty weird 32 years.
And it weren't up to me, none of it.
No choice of two roads; if there were,
       I don't doubt I'd have chosen both.
I like to think *chance* had it I play the bell.
The clue, perhaps, is in my unabashed declaration:
"I'm good example there's such a thing as called soul."
I love poetry because it makes me love
       and presents me life.
And of all the fires that die in me,
there's one burns like the sun;
it might not make day my personal life,
       my association with people,
       or my behavior toward society,
but it does tell me my soul has a shadow.

Danse Russe

WILLIAM CARLOS WILLIAMS

If when my wife is sleeping
and the baby and Kathleen
are sleeping
and the sun is a flame-white disc
in silken mists
above shining trees,—
if I in my north room
dance naked, grotesquely
before my mirror
waving my shirt round my head
and singing softly to myself:
"I am lonely, lonely.
I was born to be lonely,
I am best so!"
If I admire my arms, my face,
my shoulders, flanks, buttocks
against the yellow drawn shades,—

Who shall say I am not
the happy genius of my household?

Nelly Myers

A. R. AMMONS

I think of her
            while having a bowl of wheatflakes
(why? we never had wheatflakes
or any cereal then
except breakfast grits)
            and tears come to my eyes
and I think that I will die
because

            the bright, clear days when she was with me
and when we were together
(without caring that we were together)

can never be restored:
            my love wide-ranging
    I mused with clucking hens
and brought in from summer storms
at midnight the thrilled cold chicks
            and dried them out
            at the fireplace
and got up before morning
unbundled them from the piles of rags and
    turned them into the sun:

        I cannot go back
        I cannot be with her again

and my love included the bronze
sheaves of broomstraw
she would be coming across the fields with
before the household was more than stirring out to pee

and there she would be coming
    as mysteriously from a new world
and she was already old when I was born but I love
the thought of her hand
wringing the tall tuft of dried grass

        and I cannot see her beat out the fuzzy bloom
again
readying the straw for our brooms at home,
I can never see again the calm sentence of her mind
    as she
measured out brooms for the neighbors and charged
a nickel a broom:

I think of her
    but cannot remember how I thought of her
as I grew up: she was not a member of the family:
I knew she was not my mother,
            not an aunt, there was nothing
visiting about her: she had her room,
    she kept her bag of money
(on lonely Saturday afternoons
    you could sometimes hear the coins
spilling and spilling into her apron):
    she never went away, she was Nelly Myers, we
    called her Nel,
small, thin, her legs wrapped from knees to ankles
in homespun bandages: she always had the soreleg
                        and sometimes
red would show at the knee, or the ankle would swell
and look hot
    (and sometimes the cloths would
dwindle,

the bandages grow thin, the bowed legs look
pale and dry—I would feel good then,
          maybe for weeks
                    there would seem reason of promise,
     though she rarely mentioned her legs
and was rarely asked about them) : she always went,

legs red or white, went, went
through the mornings before sunrise
                    covering the fields and
woods
looking for huckleberries
or quieting some wild call to move and go
          roaming the woods and acres of daybreak
and there was always a fire in the stove
when my mother rose (which was not late) :

     my grandmother, they say, took her in
when she was a stripling run away from home
(her mind was not perfect
     which is no bar to this love song
               for her smile was sweet,
     her outrage honest and violent)
and they say that after she worked all day her relatives
would throw a handful of dried peas into her lap
               for her supper
and she came to live in the house I was born in the
northwest room of:

oh I will not end my grief
          that she is gone, I will not end my singing;
my songs like blueberries
felt-out and black to her searching fingers before light
welcome her
wherever her thoughts ride with mine, now or in any time
     that may come
when I am gone; I will not end visions of her naked feet

in the sandpaths: I will hear her words
      "Applecandy" which meant Christmas,
"Lambesdamn" which meant Goddamn (she was forthright
        and didn't go to church
   and nobody wondered if she should

and I agree with her the Holcomb pinegrove bordering our
field was
more hushed and lovelier than cathedrals
   not to mention country churches with unpainted boards
and so much innocence as she carried in her face
has entered few churches in one person)

and her exclamation "Founshy-day!" I know no meaning for
but knew she was using it right:

and I will not forget how though nearly deaf
she heard the tender blood in lips of children
and knew the hurt
   and knew what to do:

and I will not forget how I saw her last, tied in a chair
lest she rise to go
and fall
      for how innocently indomitable
   was her lust
and how her legs were turgid with still blood as she sat
and how real her tears were as I left
   to go back to college (damn all colleges):
      oh where her partial soul, as others thought,
roams roams my love,
mother, not my mother, grandmother, not my grandmother,
slave to our farm's work, no slave I would not stoop to:
I will not end my grief, earth will not end my grief,
I move on, we move on, some scraps of us together,
   my broken soul leaning toward her to be touched,
listening to be healed.

Family Portrait

PATRICIA GOEDICKE

Nobody here but us birds
Nobody nobody
But Father (the old crow)
Sister my blue jay
Mother my brown dove
And I
The ugly duckling with a feather
Gummed in its one weeping eye.

Like a cold critic,
An awkward spy,
I inspect the warm house,
I would snap up their hearts,
But see, my confederate
Sister blue jay
Even before I speak
Flashes bright blue away.

My crow condescends
But I shiver and shiver
Longing to share a feather,
To be framed, to flock
Together into the nest,
Yet ugly as sin,
Keeping my camera eye without,
Why should I be let in?

Only my dumpling dove
My mother my mother
She will move over
To give me cover,
And under her warm wing
I shall live on and on
I shall be white
And beautiful as a swan.

Name and Place
(For Howard Tiger, Newark, 1976)

MADELINE TIGER BASS

My father tells me he believed
men would not be different from each other,
Jew from Gentile, by the time he was old;
my father climbed all over greening Abe Lincoln
sitting there big and bronze in front of the fearful
courthouse among pigeons and tenement fires.
My father said he looked up to the hills,
he was a happy boy with no money, his violin,
his strudel kitchen, his prank strings
October nights on Belmont Avenue, his father
chuckling home with pockets and
little white paperbags of sweetcakes Saturdays.
My father said a kitchen always rang tomato soup,
families are loyal even when Tiger gambled,
left them stitch poor with Elsie in the attic
fixing patterns, the others near spinsters.
My father told me he was American he worked
hard he made it land of opportunity up hill
Hallowe'en bonfires long since and even though
it was hard to find the house on Fairmont Avenue,
still we knew the name "Tiger" was in the lintel,
the name that old tailor took landing in
this place and before he went gambling,
the name he left them, the lost name,
the name of no sons and no grandsons

If you have a land
and you know the color of the soil
wet in your hands and it has been
your father's land and his father's

before him through the thick dis-
comfort of crude shoes tromping
marking the middle of some great
continent, if it had been so
for generations, then
even if it was not given
by feudal apportionment,
even if your family's name
was only written on pain
and the government doesn't know
how they came, how long tolerated,
how tithed, even if it had not been
their land except by knowledge and
certain colors early in the morning
out past the fields, certain
sweetness of straw, spring wine
sipped in a young girl's mouth or
a sense of dig, and sleep
past seasons, past the deaths
of women in childbirth; if
you have even a crumb of such a story,
of such a land, then
it doesn't matter if you are not a man
to give a name
to your father's name
to do his labor
under this name
in the new city
to engrave this name
on the lintel of houses
to write this name
in a black Bible
to pronounce this name
in a new language
to grow old in its shade
to recognize your father

to nominate him
when you are the elder
in this name;
to present him with sons.

If there is a land
you walked in together
or a stand of blue spruce and gnarled pine
you watched together
and he told you about the saplings,
your name matters less: you can be
a daughter who does not exist
for the sake of a name.

But we have come
washed out of history,
escaped or banished, the cause indifferent,
our parts dispersed
long before we knew a homeland
long after we knew a homeland
furrowed with familiar trees,
with no connection to our fathers' steps
on earth unanchored to streets and sidewalks.
We've come with only the glittering hopes:
the wild new alphabet
in a girl's notebook,
the long brown hair of buxom peasants
with strong arms and brave tongues,
the ancient love-moon behind shops
and a cold sun to cut out the days,
to make the cement seem to shine
gold and silver. Johanna Rose dreamed,
cooking and saving, giving birth,
and starting ocean stories
hundreds of times over, to carve
at last the new name over the door

of a house in Newark, to mark our place,
to pray for sons. We have only
this amazing passage.

I have no roots in soil or language,
I have no place to dig for my caul,
only skyline and pavement of a steel city
to look back on and know
for the name's sake
to know my father
whose name is wasting,
to give him a land.

Venus in the Tropics

LOUIS SIMPSON

1

One morning when I went over to Bournemouth
it was crowded with American sailors—
chubby faces like Jack Oakie
chewing gum and cracking wise.

Pushing each other into the pool,
bellyflopping from the diving boards,
piling on the raft to sink it,
hanging from the rings, then letting go.

Later, when I went into Kingston
to exchange some library books,
they were everywhere, buying souvenirs,
calabash gourds and necklaces made of seeds.

On Saturday night at the Gaiety
they kept talking and making a noise.
When the management asked them to stop
they told it to get wise, to fly a kite, to scram.

2

We drove down to Harbor Street
with Mims ("She isn't your mother.
You ought to call her by some affectionate nickname—
why don't you call her Mims?")

There were two American cruisers,
the turrets and guns distinctly visible,
and some destroyers—I counted four.

The crews were coming ashore in launches.
As each group walked off the dock
we noticed a number of women
wearing high heels. They went up to the sailors
and engaged them in conversation.

"You've seen enough," said Mims.
"In fact, you may have seen too much."
She started the Buick, shifting into gear
swiftly with a gloved hand.

She always wore gloves and a broad hat.
To protect her complexion,
she told us. She was extremely sensitive.
All redheaded people were.

"She's a redhead, like Clara Bow,"
our father wrote in his letter.

"The Red Death," said my grandmother
twenty years later, on Eastern Parkway
in Brooklyn. We were talking about my father.
She thought he must have been ill—
not in his right mind—to marry a typist
and leave her practically everything.

How else to explain it, such an intelligent man?

3
The American warships left.
Then the *Empress of Britain*
came and stayed for a few days
during which the town was full of tourists.
Then, once more, the harbor was empty.

I sat by the pool at Bournemouth
reading *Typhoon*.
I had the pool all to myself,
the raft, the diving boards, and the rings.
There wasn't a living soul.

Not a voice—just rustling palm leaves
and the tops of the coconuts
moving around in circles.

In the afternoon a wind sprang up,
blowing from the sea to land,
covering the harbor with whitecaps.

It smelled of shells and seaweed,
and something else—perfume.

My Life

WILLIAM STAFFORD

This corridor through the air, shaped
like a person walking, is me. I follow
to here, look back a tangle that threads
where I was and might be again. When others turn
their corridor—turn it sideways or backward—
it is always there, exactly like mine,
but some have honesty right down the middle, while
mine juggles its way, twisting and trying.
I must hurry; my life is following me
around, complaining—something about rights, and
something about hope, something about yesterday.

What I Learned This Year

LEWIS WARSH

typing doesn't disturb anyone

Voices

beautiful voices
singing songs

don't disturb anyone

footsteps
on a thin wood floor

don't disturb anyone

don't disturb me
please, don't disturb me

don't disturb anyone

*

This is what I learned this year

*

golden voices

sing beautiful songs

in your ear

SHAKY   I learned
what shaky means
this year

but don't ask me

I learned that
        there are no gurus this year, but I think I always knew that

        learned what Scorpio means this year

                         but don't believe it

I've learned to believe in chronology

                it's so supporting

I learned that everyone can take of themselves this year

I learned a lot about silence

                friendship

    love

        & flowers

I learned something about destiny this year but I've forgotten
        it already

HOME

did I learn anything about home this year?

                I learned that when
          your heart said "Yes" you did it

   & that when your body said "No"
      you stopped

I learned that only love can break your heart

        but that your body can go on forever (so to speak)

I learned a little about energy, & distance

             I think I understand
        what "clairvoyance" means

I learned that people spoke metaphorically when they didn't want
    to hurt you

            & how kind they were!

I learned how people's lives connect

               & what separate means

             & the meaning of the word "useful"

                    *

I saw myself turning into my father

           & I learned a lot from that

                    *

I learned that other people's thoughts couldn't affect you

    & that it was a waste

             to think negatively about anything

I learned a little bit about ethics this year

    I thought about Charles Olson

             & Frank O'Hara a lot this year

I learned that I was hooked this year but I'm not sure to what

           I learned what being self-involved means

I learned how to ride the music, all over again

                    *

      this year

    I borrowed the lives of my brothers

I saw where my demons came from

             I learned to dig the blank spaces

I saw where not having money

    could be limiting

             in the most boring way

I looked at peace as more than a blurred possibility

    as in "peace on earth"

             or "peace of mind"

I learned that freedom's just another word

I learned that there was some other way

*

I learned what "learning to forget" meant but realized I
        secretly remembered everything

I learned that unless you stop it just goes on forever

    that unless you stop it just goes on forever

        just goes on forever

I learned that no one disturbs anyone i.e. it's all in your head

    beautiful golden voices singing in your head

*

I learned what those lights blinking in the distance meant

    what the branch brushing against the window meant

  what the writing on the wall meant, if you took it seriously

        & the sense of "inventory"

I learned what it was like to feel fresh, almost virginal,
    unembarrassed by it all

        & younger, even, than I was

The Bloody Show

JOAN MURRAY

At nineteen
the birth is early

the waters go before dark

Morn tomorrow:
the doctor says
on phone

My mother makes her pilgrimage
fearing I will not complete
this thing without her/
though our women
have a history of birth

The morning cannot wait
she says
The bloody show has come

Reluctant she leaves me
to a cab who drives
no reason
to the West Side Highway
He gets no tip

Like Bethlehem
the rooms are full
I come unfolded
to show it will be *now*

.   .   .   .   .

The doctor has not come/
The birth may not proceed
I am stored away
denied the room
to move this child from me

a nurse comes
listens to the secrets
of the fetal heart
marks an *x* on the abdomen/
does not return

I wait
touch cold tile walls
silver valves
retired operation room,
its table growing hard
narrow
alone

The pain matures

Far down the hall
a woman screams

The child cannot wait
It comes in anguish
the body taking over

Something breaks:
blood/feces lunge
at the doctor's entry

Someone clean this mess
There is no greeting

I am lifted
stretchered
wheeled to delivery
wild with the birth

The beauty of the moment
escapes
I drown in ether

.   .   .   .   .

The breasts drop milk
week on week
The doctor will not stop it

My mother mourns
the talk we never had
about this man/ my doctor
who came too late
ten years before
to bring forth her son:
She watched a nurse/ a woman
take the child from her
through a haze of ether

they told her she was wrong

In three weeks
my daughter has died
from her broken heart

A freak of nature says the doctor
There will be others

Some morning later I phone
ask him to prescribe some exercise

Just push the carriage he says

How I Changed My Name, Felice

FELIX STEFANILE

In Italy, a man's name, here a woman's,
transliterated so I went to school
for seven years, and no one told me different.
The teachers hardly cared, and in the class
Italian boys who knew me said Felice,
although outside they called me feh-LEE-tchay.

I might have lived, my noun so neutralized,
another seven years, except one day
I broke a window like nobody's girl,
and the old lady called a cop, whose sass
was wonderful when all the neighbors smiled
and said that there was no boy named Felice.
And then it was it came on me, my shame,
and I stepped up, and told him, and he grinned.

My father paid a quarter for my sin,
called me inside to look up in a book
that Felix was American for me.
A Roman name, I read. And what he said
was that no Roman broke a widow's glass,
and fanned my little neapolitan ass.

The History of My Feeling
For D.

KATHLEEN FRASER

The history of my feeling for you (or is it the way you change
and are blameless like clouds)
                         reminds me of the sky in Portland
and the morning I unpacked
and found the white plates from Iowa City
broken,
        consistently surprising with cracks,
petals like new math theories smashed
                      with the purposeful fingers of chance.
I loved the plates. They were remnants from an auction
which still goes on in my head because of the auctioneer's body
and his sexy insinuations about the goods he was selling.

But to Ruth, who talked them into their thin wraps of newspaper,
what we were sharing was departure and two lives breaking
and learning
        to mend into new forms.

We had loved our husbands,
                torn our bodies in classic ways to bear
                  children: Sammy, David, Wesley—
Now we loved new men and wept together
so that the plates weren't important and hadn't been packed
with the care I might have given had I been alone.
But Ruth was with me.

You were gone, like this storm that's been arriving and
                         disappearing
all morning.

I awoke to hear heavy rain in the gutters.
The light was uncertain and my feelings had grown less sure.
Last night, pinned by a shaft of pain—

                    your presence and your absence—
I knew clearly that I hated you
for entering me profoundly, for taking me inside you,
for husbanding me, claiming all that I knew

                          and did not know,
yet letting me go from you
into this unpredictable and loneliest of weathers.

Burning the Steaks in the Rain
Reflections on a 46th Birthday

ROBERT DANA

Age will come suddenly
the mirror says

Overnight perhaps
like a cough

And the eyes will water
the hand slow

I'm now at least thirty-five
the mirror says

But my eyes see
in their own pupils

the young boy
who's always there

Frightened
Looking

as if it were still dusk and years ago
and he

still waiting before a darkened house
its pines

porch pillars
and deep shadowed bays

Waiting still
for a glimpse of the only girl whose touch can heal

Into his
hands

this morning
not mine

the three pair of socks
dark

and dull as heartbreak
fall from their wrappings

The hand
is a hard intelligence

A lover of contradictions
should a dull gift matter

At noon
my young son calls long distance

In the evening
my daughters

They say
Father we remembered

And home from work
my second wife

kisses me
from my thick neurotic sleep

Beyond the windows
the wind runs the high grass

Silvery
Wavering

Then rushing
in long sweeps

We sit and watch it and think of fire
or the sea

Evening
on the dark lake

The last boat
growls toward the pier

and rain
drives the empty park

sweeping the trees
like a celebration

Nevertheless
the steaks are burning

Over your cloth
of red and yellow flowers

the gift of my desires
opens

Wife
I want to grow up at last

I want patience
the passion of my children

I want to learn your name
for wild Iris

I want to walk again
by the sea

I want two friends
you   and one other

I want to love you
in a field of lightning

to risk death
on your body

I want to live
another long year

Zimmer in Grade School

PAUL ZIMMER

In grade school I wondered
Why I had been born
To wrestle in the ashy puddles,
With my square nose
Streaming mucus and blood,
My knuckles puffed from combat
And the old nun's ruler.
I feared everything: God,
Learning and my schoolmates.
I could not count, spell or read.
My report card proclaimed
These scarlet failures.
My parents wrang their loving hands.
My guardian angel wept constantly.

But I could never hide anything.
If I peed my pants in class
The puddle was always quickly evident,
My worst mistakes were at
The blackboard for Jesus and all
The saints to see.
                    Even now
When I hide behind elaborate mask
It is always known that I am Zimmer,
The one who does the messy papers
And fractures all his crayons,
Who spits upon the radiators
And sits all day in shame
Outside the office of the principal.

Sabbatical

JULIA RANDALL

In general I dislike cleaning house, taking stock,
rearranging the office. It's nice when it's done,
but doing it takes such a long time. This year I finally collected
three boxes for the Goodwill, plus some worn-out suitcases.
But they wouldn't call, so I
got in touch with the Salvation Army. Now there's space
to breathe in. I am forty-three.
Years haven't heaped anything on me.
I even sold the Steinway. What was the point,
with three keys gone, and one finger-joint
stiff as a rail? I don't think
it was failure or laziness always to repeat
the same sonata, always to stare at the same mess
in the closet. The dust has a business
which the dust doesn't know. I will never (the dust tells me)
play the piano. I will never write
the article on Tennyson. I will never have children. I will never go
to Greece. I will never see
my mother again, or Brownie.

On the other hand, I have finally gotten some peace.
A cleared house looks like a lessening. But the clothes
we kept hanging around, thought we might wear sometime,
or the ones we've outgrown—everybody knows getting rid of them
is no such thing. Now I concentrate
the party dress on the left, the school on the right,
and jeans I don't bother to put away: one set on the chair,
one set in the laundry. And where
I used to stack up books from the library,
I keep a flower or two: rosemary
for remembrance, goat's rue—

And soar into clean air
like a transplant or new shoot
from the mother-root, or like a bush grown thick
from cutting back. But my bloom
will fail me, and I dread
another start-of-term. Not all my dead
approve me. I've mislaid
my Modern Novel notes, and I'm afraid
the Valley Cleaners lost my winter coat.
I mustn't forget to bring the dahlia-root
inside. This year the golden ones look good.

The Twins

CHARLES BUKOWSKI

he hinted at times that I was a bastard and I told him to listen
to Brahms, and I told him to learn to paint and drink and not be
dominated by women and dollars
but he screamed at me, For Christ's sake remember your mother,
remember your country,
you'll kill us all! . . .

I move through my father's house (on which he owes
    $8,000 after 20
years on the same job) and look at his dead shoes
the way his feet curled the leather as if he were angry planting
    roses,
and he was, and I look at his dead cigarette, his last cigarette
and the last bed he slept in that night, and I feel I should remake it
but I can't, for a father is always your master even when he's
    gone;
I guess these things have happened time and again but I can't help
thinking
    to die on a kitchen floor at 7 o'clock in the morning
    while other people are frying eggs
    is not so rough
    unless it happens to you.

I go outside and pick an orange and peel back the bright skin;
things are still living: the grass is growing quite well,
the sun sends down its rays circled by a Russian satellite;
a dog barks senselessly somewhere, the neighbors peek
    behind blinds:

I am a stranger here, and have been (I suppose) somewhat
    the rogue,
and I have no doubt he painted me quite well (the old boy and I
fought like mountain lions) and they say he left it all to
    some woman
in Duarte but I don't give a damn—she can have it: he was
    my old
man
        and he died.

inside, I try on a light blue suit
much better than anything I have ever worn
and I flap the arms like a scarecrow in the wind
but it's no good:
I can't keep him alive
no matter how much we hated each other.

we looked exactly alike, we could have been twins
the old man and I: that's what they
said. he had his bulbs on the screen
ready for planting
while I was laying with a whore from 3rd street.

very well. grant us this moment: standing before a mirror
in my dead father's suit
waiting also
to die.

Things to Do Around Taos

KEN MC CULLOUGH

Get up after a nightmare in which some dead men have
    your house surrounded
Wash thoroughly, chant, meditate, do yoga
Eat a lot of yogurt and bananas
Write twelve letters and look over the rough draft of the
    short story you're working on
Put a little cognac in your coffee and pretend you're
    an aristocrat
Walk into town and go stand around the plaza in your
    black hat pretending you are Billy Jack
Hope that Dennis Hopper sees you and puts you in his
    next paranoid movie
Pay a dollar at the La Fonda Hotel to see D. H. Lawrence's
    dirty paintings, or think about it, anyway
Pay fifty cents to go through the Kit Carson House
Be amazed when you find room after room having
    nothing to do with Kit Carson
Read about what Kit Carson did to the Navajos' peach
    orchards;
Plan to desecrate his grave
Plan to make a pilgrimage to Blue Lake if you can get
    permission
Plan to make pilgrimages to Mesa Verde, Canyon de
    Chelly, Chaco Canyon and Oraibi
Plan to do Sufi dancing some Sunday out at the Lama
    Foundation
Go into the shop next to the Kit Carson House
Have the woman who runs it follow you around to
    make sure you don't rip anything off
Go to the bookstore across the street run by a woman
    with cruel eyes

114

Buy one book, rip off two
Go to the Harwood Library and look at the death carts
    upstairs
Walk to the Post Office in the late afternoon to get your
    mail
Drop in at Dori's Bakery
Curse Dori's jovial face as you sit there eating pastry
    after pastry
Start home, get splattered with mud by some redneck
    in a pickup just as you're admiring your picture
    on a poster of a contest you've just won
Get home and do some more chanting, some more yoga
Read *The Penitentes of the Southwest*
Sit in the yard with your shirt off feeding crackers to
    the sparrows
Watch a magpie beat up on a solitary sparrow
Go to the laundromat and do clothes
Forget to turn the knob from "cold" to "hot"
Be the last one out as the lovely senoritas sweep up
Have fantasies about them as they lean over in their
    tight jeans
Go home and dress up entirely in black
Go to La Cocina and drink brandy, hoping a rich young
    widow will see you, be impressed, and say let me
    take you home with me and be your Sugar Mom
Make eyes at the cocktail waitress
Check out her profile against the fluorescent lights
Imagine skinny-dipping with her on a moonlit night
    out at the hot springs in The Gorge
Give a skier hard looks when he catches you perusing
    his bunny
Be awkward when some lady asks you if you've found
    Zoot Finley yet
Be embarrassed when a member of the group playing
    nods a friendly hello
Wish it was summer

Hear from everybody that D. H. Lawrence was the
     biggest fascist that ever lived
Go across the street and hear Antonio entertain the
     turista
Stand next to a couple from Denver and develop instant
     rapport
Dance a flamenco with Benjamin, drunk simpatico
     from the pueblo
Tell the couple your life story
Bid goodbye to Benjamin in his blanket as he is being
     tossed out
Go to Los Compadres and be the only Anglo there,
Finish your beer and leave in a hurry
Go to a dance at Casa Loma,
Feel like a child molester
Go back to La Cocina and ask the cocktail waitress if
     she'd like to go for a drink at Antonio's
She says yes, you go, she finishes half the drink and
     leaves in a hurry
Talk to the guy you're left standing next to about Ireland
Go to the Men's Room and notice you still have a big
     glop of mud in your left ear
Make a date with the barmaid with no intention of
     keeping it
Sneak out and get splattered by some mestizo high
     school kids
Get in your mud-splattered battered car, drive home,
     find the phone number of a friend in New Orleans,
     drive out to a freezing phone booth
Punch the phone when it eats your only dime
Drive home again in a swoon and go off the road into
     a snowbank
Leave the car and walk home to leftover black-eyed peas,
a cold bed, and the dead men surrounding your house

Orange

VI GALE

Once the long season had us in its reach
our miracles were few. On the Christmas Eve
that an uncle came traveling, traveling on skis
with the gift of an orange, my brother and I
went wild in our marveling.

We held the unbelievable in hand
there as we pared and shared and hoarded peel.
We had the summer as our guest
for *Jul* there as we feasted. Florida, Fresno, and gold
rivaled the night's candleshine.

Halfway around the world one later December
on a day so mild that we'd sunned in Los Angeles,
I reached easily into boughs, into rich leaves;
pulled out a childhood of long snow,
the far sound of skis.

BIOGRAPHICAL NOTES

Biographical Notes

A. R. Ammons (b. 1926) was born in Whiteville, North Carolina. He served in the United States Naval Reserve (in the South Pacific) from 1944 to 1946, and was graduated from Wake Forest College in 1949 with a B.S. degree. He was the poetry editor of *The Nation* in 1963 and has taught at Cornell University since 1964. In 1973 he was awarded a National Book Award for his COLLECTED POEMS (1972).

Jim Barnes (b. 1933) is of Choctaw-Welsh-English ancestry. He has a Ph.D. in Comparative Literature from the University of Arkansas (1972). His poetry and translations have appeared in numerous magazines and in major anthologies. He has been the poetry editor of *Places*, and is the editor of *Chariton Review*, published by Northeast Missouri State University, where he is a teacher.

Madeline Tiger Bass (b. 1934) was born in New York City. She graduated from Wellesley College with a B.A. degree in 1956, and received her M.A.T. from Harvard University in 1957. In addition to being a mother of five children, she teaches in the Artists-in-the-Schools program of the New Jersey State Council on the Arts, is on the staff of Upward Bound at Seton Hall University, and at Bergen Community College, Division of Community Services. She is the recipient of a New Jersey State Council on the Arts 1977–1978 Fellowship grant for poetry writing and study. Her first book of poems, KEEPING THE HOUSE IN THIS FOREST, was published in 1977.

Marvin Bell (b. 1937) was born in New York City. He holds a B.A. from Alfred University (1958) and an M.A. from the University of Chicago (1961). He has been teaching poetry workshops at the University of Iowa since 1965. He was the poetry editor of *North American Review* from 1964 to 1969, and of the *Iowa Review* from 1969 to 1971. His books of poems include A PROBABLY VOLUME OF DREAMS (1969) and RESIDUE OF SONG (1974).

Paul Blackburn (1927–1971) had a varied career as a writer, editor, and translator. He was the poetry editor of *The Nation* in 1962, a poet-in-residence on two occasions, and the recipient of both the Fulbright and Guggenheim fellowships. His translations of Provencal poetry are said to be the best in the English language. THE CITIES (1967) is a collection of

121

most of the poems he wrote before that year. EARLY SELECTED Y MAS: COLLECTED POEMS, 1949–1961, was published shortly after his death.

Allan Block (b. 1923) was born in Oshkosh, Wisconsin. He attended the University of Wisconsin, 1939–1941, and Columbia University, 1945–1946. He was the owner of a sandal and leather-craft store in New York from 1950 to 1969. In 1969 he moved to an old farmhouse in New Hampshire, where he manages to make a successful living as a leather worker, farmer, poet, and Saturday night square dance fiddler. His one full-length book of poems is entitled IN NOAH'S WAKE (1972).

Harold Bond (b. 1939) was born in Boston, Massachusetts. He received his A.B. degree from Northeastern University (Boston) in 1962, and his M.F.A. from the University of Iowa in 1967. He teaches poetry writing at the Cambridge Center for Adult Education. His work has appeared in numerous anthologies, and he is the author of two poetry collections: THE NORTHERN WALL (1969) and DANCING ON WATER (1970).

David Bottoms (b. 1949) was born in Canton, Georgia. He holds a B.A. from Mercer University (1971) and an M.A. from West Georgia College (1973). His poems have appeared in a number of important magazines and in anthologies. He is the editor of a series of pamphlets by Southern poets (Burnt Hickory Press). He has worked in the Georgia Poets-in-the-Schools program, and is an avid Bluegrass musician. His instruments are banjo and guitar.

John Brandi (b. 1943) was born in Los Angeles, California. He graduated from California State College with a B.F.A. in 1965. He was a member of the Peace Corps from 1965 to 1968, serving in South America. He is a painter as well as a poet, and has exhibited his work in the United States and Mexico. In addition to his books of poetry, he has also published volumes of short stories and travel journals.

Charles Bukowski (b. 1920) was born in Andernach, Germany, of an American father and German mother. He did not begin writing poetry until he was thirty-five. For years he worked as a post office clerk and mailman, but in recent years he has been able to devote his full time to writing. His books include works of fiction and nonfiction, but he is best known for his poetry. His most representative collection of poems is THE DAYS RUN AWAY LIKE WILD HORSES OVER THE HILLS (1969).

Lucille Clifton (b. 1936) was born in Depew, New York. She married Fred J. Clifton, educator-writer-artist, in 1958, and they have six children. She has had several civil service jobs and has been the poet-in-residence at Coppin State College in Baltimore since 1971. She has published several books of poems, as well as a number of books for children.

122

Gregory Corso (b. 1930) was born in New York City. He was raised by foster parents in New York in poverty and violence. It was after serving a three-year prison sentence that he met Allen Ginsberg, who encouraged his gift for poetry. He has held a variety of jobs and is widely traveled. He is one of the three avowed "Beat" poets, and his best-known books are GASOLINE (1958), THE HAPPY BIRTHDAY OF DEATH (1960), and LONG LIVE MAN (1962).

Robert Dana (b. 1929) was born in Allston, Massachusetts. He received his A.B. degree from Drake University in 1951 and his M.A. from the University of Iowa in 1953. He is professor of English at Cornell College. He served in the United States Navy, 1946–1948, and was the editor of *North American Review*, 1964–1968. Among his five books of poems are SOME VERSIONS OF SILENCE (1967) and THE RIVER OF THE INVISIBLE (1971).

Rosemary Daniell (b. 1935) is a native of Atlanta, Georgia. She is a mother of three, and has worked as a journalist, advertising copywriter, poetry reviewer, poetry workshop teacher, and as a program director for Georgia's Poets-in-the-Schools program. Her first book of poems, A SEXUAL TOUR OF THE DEEP SOUTH, won critical acclaim.

Ann Darr (b. 1920) was born in Bagley, Iowa, a town of six hundred. She received her undergraduate degree from the University of Iowa in 1941. After college she moved to New York, where she wrote and performed radio scripts for N.B.C. and A.B.C. During World War II she served with the Women's Air Force Service Pilots. She now lives with her family outside Washington, D.C. She is a recipient of a Discovery 70 Award from the Poetry Center of New York, and the author of THE MYTH OF A WOMAN'S FIST (1973) and ST. ANN'S GUT (1971).

R. P. Dickey (b. 1936) was born in Flat River, Missouri. He served in the United States Air Force from 1954 to 1956. He attended the University of Missouri, where he received his B.A. degree in 1968 and his M.A. in 1969. He has taught creative writing at several colleges and has traveled widely to give readings of his poems. He was the founding editor of *Poetry Bag Press*. His books of poems include RUNNING LUCKY (1969) and ACTING IMMORTAL (1970).

Rhoda Donovan (b. 1946) was born in the Bronx, New York. She received her B.A. in English in 1968 from the State University of New York at Albany. She also attended the University of Arizona, where she received her M.A. in English in 1970 and her M.F.A. in Creative Writing in 1973. She has been an assistant professor of English at the Vermont College Division of Norwich University since 1974. She has published her poems in numerous little magazines.

D. W. Donzella (b. 1951) was born in Bridgeport, Connecticut. He graduated from the University of Connecticut in 1972. He has lived in Bridgeport all his life, and has worked at various odd jobs: mechanic, sales clerk, substitute teacher, and, since 1974, in the Connecticut Poets-in-the-Schools program. His poetry and fiction have appeared in a number of magazines and he was awarded a grant from the Connecticut Arts Commission to work on a novel.

Alan Dugan (b. 1923) was born in Brooklyn, New York. He graduated from Mexico City College in 1950. He has taught at Connecticut College, Sarah Lawrence, and the Fine Arts Center in Provincetown, Massachusetts. He was awarded both the Pulitzer Prize and a National Book Award in 1962 for POEMS OF ALAN DUGAN (1961). His COLLECTED POEMS appeared in 1969.

Edward Field (b. 1924) was born in Brooklyn, New York. He served in the United States Army Air Force from 1942 to 1946. His first book, STAND UP, FRIEND, WITH ME, was the Lamont Poetry Selection in 1962. His other books of poetry are VARIETY PHOTOPLAYS (1967) and A FULL HEART (1977). He often performs with amateur acting groups and he has traveled widely to give readings of his poems. He was awarded a Guggenheim Fellowship in 1963.

Kathleen Fraser (b. 1937) was born in Tulsa, Oklahoma. She graduated from Occidental College with a B.A. in 1959. She taught for two years at the University of Iowa Writer's Workshop before taking a one-year post as a Writer-in-Residence at Reed College. She has taught at San Francisco State College since 1972. Her major collections of poetry are WHAT I WANT (1974) and NEW SHOES: OR WHY I CROSS OUT WORDS (1978).

Vi Gale (b. 1917) was born in Noret, Dala-Jarna, Sweden. She taught writing at the Portland Y.W.C.A. from 1962 to 1972. In 1974 she established the Prescott Street Press, which has as its concern regional publishing in fine editions. She has published poetry, short stories, articles, and her own photographs. Her three full-length books are SEVERAL HOUSES (1959), LOVE ALWAYS (1965), and CLEARWATER (1974). She has taught at literary conferences and seminars and has been a participant and organizer for the Portland Poetry Festival.

Isabella Gardner (b. 1915) was born in Newton, Massachusetts. She attended several acting schools in the 1930s, including Leighton Rollins School of Acting in East Hampton, New York, and the Embassy School of Acting in London. She has worked as a professional actor and as a reader for publishers. She was associate editor, with Karl Shapiro, of *Poetry* from 1952 to 1956. Her books of poems include WEST OF CHILDHOOD: POEMS 1950–65 (1965).

Jim Gibbons (b. 1944) was born in Milwaukee, Wisconsin. He has worked in the post office in Sausalito, California (where he lived on a houseboat), has taught creative writing in high schools, and worked with CETA, the Federal government's Comprehensive Employment and Training Act. He is now a labor crew leader in Ukiah, California. His book of poems, PRIME THE PUMP, was published in 1970, and two other books, MUD GRUNGE and BORN IN MILWAUKEE, are awaiting publication.

Patricia Goedicke grew up in Hanover, New Hampshire, and now lives with her novelist husband in San Miguel de Allende, Guanajuato, Mexico. She has taught at Ohio State University, Hunter College, and the Institute Allende. Her first published poem appeared in the *Kenyon Review* in 1956 and her first book of poems, BETWEEN OCEANS, was published in 1968. She is also the author of THE TRAIL THAT TURNS ON ITSELF (1978) and NEW LETTERS for which she received the 1976 William Carlos Williams prize for poetry.

Alfred Starr Hamilton (b. 1914) was born in Montclair, New Jersey, where he has lived a good part of his life as a semi-recluse. He served in the United States Army from 1942 to 1943. He has hitchhiked through forty-three states. His one book, titled POEMS OF ALFRED STARR HAMILTON, was published in 1970.

Richard Hugo (b. 1923) was born in Seattle, Washington. He graduated from the University of Washington with a B.A. in 1948 and received an M.A. in 1952. He served in the United States Army Air Force from 1943 to 1945. He has been a member of the department of English at the University of Montana since 1964. He was awarded a Rockefeller Foundation creative writing grant in 1967. His books of poems include THE LADY IN KICKING HORSE RESERVOIR (1973) and WHAT THOU LOVEST WELL REMAINS AMERICAN (1975).

Colette Inez (b. 1931) was born in Brussels, Belgium. She received a B.A. from Hunter College in 1961. She has worked for various magazines, has taught high school and poetry workshops, and has been a book reviewer and poetry translator. Her book of poems, THE WOMAN WHO LOVED WORMS, was published in 1972 and another, ALIVE AND TAKING NAMES, in 1977. She lives in New York City, where she conducts a poetry workshop at the New School for Social Research.

David Kherdian (b. 1931) was born in Racine, Wisconsin. He graduated from the University of Wisconsin with a B.S. in 1960. He worked as a bookseller and bibliographer before becoming a poet at the age of thirty-five. He is the author of SIX SAN FRANCISCO POETS (1969) and the editor of a number of contemporary American poetry anthologies. He was the founder-editor of The Giligia Press (1967–1974). His books of poems include THE NONNY POEMS (1974), ANY DAY OF YOUR LIFE (1975), and I REMEMBER ROOT RIVER (1978).

Ronald Koertge (b. 1940) was born in Olney, Illinois. He graduated from the University of Illinois with a B.A. in 1962, and he received his M.A. in English from the University of Arizona in 1965. He worked in a packing plant, on farms, and as a salesman in department stores, before becoming an English teacher at Pasadena City College, a position he has held since 1965. He has published seven books and chapbooks of poetry, most notably, THE FATHER POEMS (1973).

Phyllis Koestenbaum (b. 1930) was born in Brooklyn, New York. She graduated from Radcliffe College in 1952, and is working for a Master's Degree in Creative Writing at San Francisco State University. Although she didn't begin writing poetry until she was forty-four years old, her poems have since been published in magazines and in two anthologies. She is married and the mother of four children.

Stephen Shu Ning Liu (b. 1930) was born in China. He received his B.A. in Chinese Literature at Nanking University. He came to America in 1952 as a student, and he holds an M.A. from the University of Texas (1959) and a Ph.D. from the University of North Dakota (1973), the same year he became a United States citizen. Since 1973 he has been teaching World Literature and Creative Writing at Clark Community College in Las Vegas, Nevada. His poems and translations have been widely published in magazines and anthologies.

Freya Manfred (b. 1944) was born in Minneapolis, Minnesota. She is the daughter of Frederick Manfred, the novelist. She graduated from Macalester College with a B.A. in 1966, and has an M.A. in English (1968) from Stanford University. She has worked in the Poets-in-the-Schools program since 1972. In 1975–1976 she was the Radcliffe Fellow in Poetry. Her work has appeared in a number of magazines and anthologies, and she is the author of A GOLDENROD WILL GROW (1971) and YELLOW SQUASH WOMAN (1977).

Ken McCullough (b. 1943) was born in Staten Island, New York. He graduated from the University of Delaware with a B.A. in 1966 and from the University of Iowa with an M.F.A. in 1968. He has taught at Montana State College, and is now a Writer-in-Residence for the South Carolina Educational Television Network, where he works on documentaries, adaptations, and his own dramatic scripts. His books of poetry include EASY WRECKAGE (1971) and CREOSOTE (1976).

Thomas McGrath (b. 1916) was born near Sheldon, North Dakota. After receiving his undergraduate degree he attended New College, Oxford, as a Rhodes Scholar from 1947 to 1948. He has written documentary and animated films and several low-budget features, and he is the

126

former editor of *Crazy Horse* magazine. He has also written juveniles and a novel. His major poetic work is LETTER TO AN IMAGINARY FRIEND (Vol. I, 1962; Vol. II, 1970). His shorter poems were collected in THE MOVIE AT THE END OF THE WORLD: SELECTED POEMS (1964).

Ann Menebroker (b. 1936) was born in Washington, D.C. She has worked as a clerk typist, a luncheon hostess, and she has taught poetry to first and second graders. Her poetry has been appearing in little magazines for more than twenty years. She has published five chapbooks of poetry, including FIVE DRUMS FOR THE LADY (1973), and since 1975 she has been the co-editor of *Wine Rings*, a magazine.

Susan Mernit (b. 1953) was born in New York and is a graduate of Bard College (1974). She teaches English at Ohio State University and works in the Ohio Poets-in-the-Schools program. She has worked as a library assistant, camp counselor, and street musician. Her poems have appeared in magazines and anthologies and she is the author of THE ANGELIC ALPHABET (1976). She is the editor of *Hand Book*, a magazine.

Robert Mezey (b. 1935) was born in Philadelphia. He graduated from the University of Iowa in 1959 with a B.A. degree. He was awarded the Lamont Poetry Award in 1960 for THE LOVEMAKER. He is a translator and anthologist as well as a poet, and teaches in the English Department of Pomona College. His books and chapbooks of poems include THE DOOR STANDING OPEN: NEW AND SELECTED POEMS, 1954–1969 (1970).

Joan Murray (b. 1945) was born in the Bronx, New York. She has been an instructor at Lehman College (City University of New York) and has taught visual arts to young people. She is a teacher in the Pennsylvania Poets-in-the-Schools program. She is also an associate editor of Sunbury Press. Her work has appeared in numerous magazines and she has published a book of poems, EGG TOOTH (1975). Her fiction is included in IN THE LOOKING GLASS (Putnam, 1977).

Frank O'Hara (1926–1966) was born in Baltimore, Maryland. He received a B.A. from Harvard University (1950) and an M.A. (1951) from the University of Michigan. He worked for *Art News* from 1953 to 1955, and was associate curator of the Museum of Modern Art in New York from 1955 until his accidental death in 1966. In addition to being a poet, he was a playwright and the author of a series of monographs on contemporary artists. He won the Hopwood Award for poetry in 1951, and his COLLECTED POEMS, published in 1971, was awarded a National Book Award.

Marge Piercy (b. 1936) was born in Detroit, Michigan. She graduated from the University of Michigan with an A.B. in 1957, and she received her M.A. from Northwestern University in 1958. She is a member of the Feminist Party and she was an activist in the revolutionary movement among young Americans in the 1960s. She is a novelist as well as a poet, and she frequently gives readings of her works. Her poetry books include BREAKING CAMP (1968), TO BE OF USE (1973), and LIVING IN THE OPEN (1976).

Julia Randall (b. 1923) was born in Baltimore, Maryland. She graduated from Bennington College with a B.A. in 1945, and holds an M.A. from Johns Hopkins University (1950). Since 1962 she has taught at a number of colleges, and she has worked as a librarian and biological technician. She was awarded a grant by the American Academy of Arts and Letters in 1968. Her books of poetry include THE PURITAN CARPENTER (1965) and ADAM'S DREAM (1969).

David Ray (b. 1932) graduated with a B.A. from the University of Chicago in 1952 and received an M.A. from the same university in 1957. He teaches English at the University of Missouri and has taught at numerous other colleges. He has been the editor of *New Letters* magazine since 1971, and has edited anthologies. His books of poems include X RAYS, A BOOK OF POEMS (1965), DRAGGING THE MAIN (1968), and GATHERING FIREWOOD: NEW AND SELECTED POEMS (1974).

William Pitt Root (b. 1941) was born in Austin, Minnesota. He graduated from the University of Washington with a B.A. in 1964, and received his M.F.A. from the University of North Carolina in 1967. He worked at a series of odd jobs before becoming a professional writer and teacher. He has taught English, been a Lecturer in Writing, and a visiting Writer-in-Residence at several colleges and universities. His books of poetry include THE STORM AND OTHER POEMS (1969), STRIKING THE DARK AIR FOR MUSIC (1973), and COOT AND OTHER CHARACTERS (1977).

Aram Saroyan (b. 1943) began his career with one-word and one-line poems that he referred to as "visual and verbal puns." His two major collections during this period were ARAM SAROYAN (1968) and PAGES (1969). His more traditional works are THE STREET: AN AUTOBIOGRAPHICAL NOVEL (1974) and O MY GENERATION (1976), a collection of poems. He was the publisher and editor of *Lines* magazine, 1964–1965, and is the editor of Blackberry Books.

Anne Sexton (1928–1974) was born in Newton, Massachusetts. She was a fashion model (1950–1951) and she achieved immediate fame on publication of her first book, TO BEDLAM AND PART WAY BACK (1960). She received numerous grants and awards and traveled around the country reading her poems. Her SELECTED POEMS appeared in 1964. She was married and the mother of two children.

Naomi Shihab (b. 1952) was born in St. Louis, Missouri. She graduated in 1974 from Trinity University with bachelor degrees in English and World Religions. Since 1973 she has worked in the Poets-in-the-Schools program for the Texas Commission on Arts and Humanities. A chapbook of her poems, TATTOOED FEET, was published in 1977. She is also a songwriter and singer.

Louis Simpson (b. 1923) was born in Jamaica, British West Indies. He attended Columbia University, where he received his Ph.D. in 1959. He worked as an editor at the Bobbs-Merrill Company from 1950 to 1955. Since then he has taught at Columbia University, the University of California (Berkeley), and the State University of New York, Stony Brook. He won the Pulitzer Prize in poetry in 1964 for AT THE END OF THE ROAD. He has also written plays, a novel, and his autobiography, NORTH OF JAMAICA (1972).

W. D. Snodgrass (b. 1926) was born in Wilkinsburg, Pennsylvania. He graduated from the State University of Iowa, where he received his B.A. in 1949, his M.A. in 1951, and his M.F.A. in 1953. He worked as a hotel clerk and hospital aide before becoming a college professor; and he has taught at Cornell, University of Rochester, and Wayne State University. His numerous grants and awards include the Pulitzer Prize for poetry in 1960 for HEART'S NEEDLE. He is also the author of AFTER EXPERIENCE: POEMS AND TRANSLATIONS (1968) and IN RADICAL PURSUIT: CRITICAL ESSAYS AND LECTURES (1975).

William Stafford (b. 1914) was born in the Midwest. He was a conscientious objector in World War II, an experience he has recorded in a work of nonfiction. Since 1957 he has taught English at Lewis and Clark College in Portland, Oregon. He was awarded the National Book Award in poetry in 1962 for TRAVELING THROUGH THE DARK: POEMS. He was the poetry consultant to the Library of Congress in 1970–1971. His COLLECTED POEMS was published in 1977.

Felix Stefanile (b. 1920) was born in Long Island City, New York. He has been a professor of English at Purdue University since 1969. He is the publisher and editor of *Sparrow*, a magazine which also publishes chapbooks of poetry and criticism. He has translated French and Italian poetry. His books of poetry include A FIG TREE IN AMERICA (1970) and EAST RIVER NOCTURNE (1976).

Alma Villanueva (b. 1944) was born in Lompoc, California, and grew up in San Francisco. She now lives in Sebastopol, California, with her five children. She is the author of BLOOD ROOT (1977), a book of poems, and her poetry was awarded first place in the third Chicano Literary Prize competition at the University of California at Irvine, in 1977.

Lewis Warsh (b. 1944) was born in the Bronx, New York. He attended City College, obtaining his B.S. in 1966 and his M.A. in 1975. He is co-founder and editor of Angel Hair Books, which has been publishing both a magazine and poetry books since 1966. He has worked as a teacher and translator, and among the books of poetry he has written are DREAMING AS ONE: POEMS (1971).

Philip Whalen (b. 1923) was born in Portland, Oregon. He was one of the original poets of the San Francisco Renaissance. He grew up in Oregon, but has lived in San Francisco almost continuously since graduating from Reed College in 1951. He has taught English in Japan, and now lives and works at the Zen Center in San Francisco. Among his books of poetry is ON BEAR'S HEAD (1969).

William Carlos Williams (1883–1963) was born in Rutherford, New Jersey. He completed medical school in 1909, the year his first book, POEMS, was published. His dictum, "no ideas but in things," and his poetry, essays, novels, and stories, together with his continuing support of up-and-coming poets—who looked to him for encouragement and advice—established him as the most influential creative force for the poets who have come of age in the second half of the twentieth century.

Al Young (b. 1939) was born in Ocean Springs, Mississippi. He graduated from the University of California (Berkeley) with a B.A. in 1969. He toured this country as a free-lance musician from 1959 to 1964, playing guitar and flute, and singing. He worked as a disk jockey from 1961 to 1965, and he was Jones Lecturer at Stanford University from 1969 to 1974. He has published several novels and books of poems, and since 1972 has been the co-editor of the magazine, *Yardbird Reader*. He was awarded a Guggenheim Fellowship in 1974.

Paul Zimmer (b. 1934) was born in Canton, Ohio. He has managed book stores and book departments in San Francisco. He has also been a poet-in-residence at Chico State College. He is the editor of the Pitt Poetry Series, a job he has held since 1967. His books of poems are RIBS OF DEATH (1967), THE REPUBLIC OF MANY VOICES (1969), and THE ZIMMER POEMS (1977).

INDEXES

Index to Authors

Index to Titles

Index to First Lines

I am 32 years old, 79
I am turning thirty, 4
I have been the planner, 15
I played old Country and Western, 61
I think of her, 82
I thought of you last night, 32
I walked a hangover like my death down, 58
I was not divinely inspired, 1
I will be an old woman in a red cotton dress riding
        a bicycle, 25
If when my wife is sleeping, 81
In general I dislike cleaning house, taking stock, 110
In grade school I wondered, 109
In Italy, a man's name, here a woman's, 103
In this photo, circa 1934, 76
It all happened like this: 13
It was Thanksgiving, 68

M

My father tells me he believed, 88
My mother writes from Trenton, 46

N

Nobody here but us birds, 86

O

On this day in Sicily, 48
Once the long season had us in its reach, 117
One morning when I went over to Bournemouth, 92

R

Rise at 7:15, 11
Rosemary, 60

S

Sawing the wood, 19
since grammar school i remember kids laughing, 3
So it has come to this—, 8
So youre playing, 53

Acknowledgments

Thanks are due to the following for permission to include copyrighted poems:

Atheneum Publishers, Inc., for "Verses *Versus* Verses" from *A Probable Volume of Dreams* by Marvin Bell, Copyright © 1969 by Marvin Bell (this poem appeared originally in *Poetry*); and "Song in 5 Parts" from *Striking the Dark Air for Music* by William Pitt Root, Copyright © 1973 by William Pitt Root.

Jim Barnes and University of Nebraska Press, for "These Damned Trees Crouch," reprinted from *Prairie Schooner*, vol. XLIV, no. 2, Summer 1970, and from *Carriers of the Dream Wheel* (Harper & Row, 1975).

Madeline Tiger Bass, for "Name and Place," Copyright © 1978 by Madeline Tiger Bass.

William L. Bauhan, Publisher, for "In Those Times" from *In Noah's Wake* by Allan Block, Copyright © 1972 by Allan Block.

Black Sparrow Press, for "Good Morning, Love!" from *Early Selected y Mas* by Paul Blackburn, Copyright © 1972 by Joan Blackburn; and "The Twins" from *Burning in Water, Drowning in Flame* by Charles Bukowski, Copyright © 1960 by Charles Bukowski.

Harold Bond, for "Foibles" from *The Young American Poets* (Follett/ Big Table Books, 1968); Parts I and III collected in *Dancing on Water* (The Cummington Press), Copyright © 1968, 1969 by Harold Bond.

David Bottoms, for "Jamming with the Band at the VFW" from *White Trash*, edited by Nancy Stone and Robert Waters Grey, published by New South Company, 1976.

Corinth Books, for "What I Learned This Year" from *Dreaming as One* by Lewis Warsh, Copyright © 1971 by Lewis Warsh.

John Brandi, for "Turning 30 Poems," Copyright © 1978 by John Brandi.

Robert Dana, for "Burning the Steaks in the Rain" (this poem appeared originally in *The North American Review*, University of Northern Iowa, Cedar Falls, Iowa 50612).

R. P. Dickey, for "Dickey in Tucson," Copyright © 1978 by R. P. Dickey.

Rhoda Donovan, for "Ten Week Wife," Copyright © 1977 by Rhoda